Best of Times

Best of Times

*More Mischief and Memories from a
Nashville Kid of the '50s*

TOM HENDERSON III

Copyright © 2017 by Tom Henderson III

www.tomhenderson3.com

First published in October 2017

ISBN-13: 978-1977905222
ISBN-10: 1977905226

Contact information:

Tom Henderson III
P.O. Box 58612
Nashville, TN 37205

tp3@comcast.net

Book design by Allen Forkum
of The Nashville Retrospect

Edited by Paul Erland

I dedicate this book to my high school English instructor at Battle Ground Academy, Mr. John Bragg, a World War II hero who defended our country by literally rooting out the Japs from their caves on the black sands of Iwo Jima in 1945—something us kids never knew. His dedicated instruction to theme composition and frequent games of "Word Wealth" recall, made his classroom one of the few in which I, even remotely, paid attention. His personal efforts to making sure I was accepted to college, when I was at best a marginal student, have never been forgotten. Thank you, Mr. Bragg, for all you did for me, and for all you did for our country.

CONTENTS

FOREWORD ix

PREFACE x

CHAPTER 1 Snow Days 1

CHAPTER 2 Scouting Days 11

CHAPTER 3 In the Mood 20

CHAPTER 4 Halloween 1959 29

CHAPTER 5 What It Was, Was Football 37

CHAPTER 6 Home Cooking 45

CHAPTER 7 The Gators 68

CHAPTER 8 The Blizzard of '51 78

CHAPTER 9 Hitchin' a Ride 87

CHAPTER 10 Saturday at the Y 95

CHAPTER 11 Fireworks 102

CHAPTER 12 Back to School 112

CHAPTER 13 An Education in Mischief 122

CHAPTER 14 Basketball Days 159

CHAPTER 15 1974 168

CHAPTER 16 Blowing Smoke 179

CHAPTER 17 Beer, Wine & Whiskey. 188

CHAPTER 18 Hideouts 205

CHAPTER 19 Old-Time Religion 213

ABOUT THE AUTHOR 222

FOREWORD

When Tom Henderson III asked me to write a foreword to his book "Best of Times," my instinctive inclination was to say "yes." I am a half-generation older than Tom and knew his father, Tom Henderson Jr., when we both worked at National Life & Accident Insurance Company. I can remember years ago, when Mr. Henderson would travel to sales meeting in Denver in the company's private plane, he would sometimes bring back a supply of Coors beer for some of us who worked in the home office and spent our lunchtimes running or playing basketball or handball at the Downtown YMCA. At the time it was illegal to buy Coors beer in Tennessee, so we were appreciative of Mr. Henderson's assistance. As a historian, I have written about the brazen attempt Tom's grandfather, Captain Tom Henderson, made in January 1919 with Colonel Luke Lea and several other Tennesseans, to capture the German Kaiser in Count Bentinct's castle in Holland.

I held back on my acceptance of Tom's request, however, until I read the manuscript. I found it interesting, particularly since it brought back many similar memories I had of growing up 14 years earlier and a few miles from the Henderson home on Cantrell Avenue. Just as Tom and his friends played in Sugartree Creek, so did I with two of my childhood friends in Richland Creek. Just as Tom escaped Sunday School at West End United Methodist Church by going down to the Elliston Place Drug Store, so I slipped up Fifth Avenue North from Sunday School, at the First Presbyterian Church, to get some refreshments before attending church.

When you read Tom's book, you will realize how relatively innocent boys and girls were in Nashville and in Franklin the 1960s and 1970s as compared to today. Most of Tom's friends neither drank nor smoked, but they did spend as much time as possible outdoors or, when in school, playing tricks on classmates and teachers—Tom at BGA, and I at MBA. We also experienced the annoyance of having to attend study hall on Saturday mornings to work off demerits that we deserved.

As I went to church with the Herbert family, I have always known about Herbert Field, where neighborhood kids played football. The comparable field for me and my schoolmates at Parmer School was the Onion Bowl, beside the Belle Meade Country Club's 14th fairway (see Tom's book "Yesterdays"). When Tom was in Woodmont School, he looked up to former Vanderbilt star football players Charlie Hoover and Bill Wade, a Woodmont graduate. Tom also admired Don McIlhenny, a great high-school halfback. McIlhenny led Hillsboro High School to its first-ever victory over MBA on MBA's homecoming weekend, winning 19-0 on Friday, Oct. 31, 1952. That evening, Hillsboro High School burned to the ground.

Tom's book has wonderful stories of his childhood adventures and many rare photographs and cartoons that readers may not have seen, including some dramatic pictures taken during the Blizzard of '51, and even one of Melfi's restaurant that I had forgotten about. The pictures add a great deal to this entertaining book. Also, in a number of his chapters, he provides a wider historical context, such as in Chapter 11, entitled "Fireworks," where he recounts the Chinese invention of fireworks 2,000 years ago before getting down to telling stories about the Black Cat firecrackers and Roman candles that he shot off as a boy. This interesting technique enhances the book, which I recommend, particularly to people who might recall Hoss Allen on WLAC, Stringbean on the Grand Ole Opry, and Owen Bradley's band playing the "Last Dance" at the Hillwood Country Club.

Ridley Wills II

Author of "Nashville Pikes, Volume One: 150 Years Along the Franklin Pike and Granny White Pike" (2015), "Nashville Pike, Volume Two: 150 Years Along the Hillsboro Pike" (2016), "Nashville Pikes, Volume Three: 150 Years Along the Harding Pike" (2017) and numerous other books about Nashville history

PREFACE

Over the past eight years I have written many stories about growing up in the 1950s and 1960s, most of which have appeared in "The Nashville Retrospect" newspaper. A lot of those involve some type of innocent mischief, because that's just who I was while navigating my way through life in those wonderful years. I am sure some of my actions and activities mirrored those of many other kids going through their early adolescence in similar towns across America. My two prior books—"When I Was a Kid" and "Yesterdays"—both reflect that.

Now comes my third book, "Best of Times." Here you will experience everything from old rock-and-roll songs, school misbehavior, shooting off fireworks, and those big snows we used to have, to trick-or-treating in 1959, hitchhiking, being a scout, streaking, and how not to behave when made to go to church. Just glance over the contents, pick a chapter, and read about a time of innocence, and of growing up in neighborhoods that are now long gone. You might even say to yourself: "Hey, I remember doing something like that. It was me and Peggy Sue, or Billy, when we got caught…" You get the picture.

Now turn the page, and let's get back to those good old days.

Best of Times

CHAPTER 1

Snow Play

ONLY TWO months after I was born, our town registered 13 inches of snow in February 1947. Clueless at that time, and for a few years after, I was at the mercy of my mother on what type of winter wear I would be clothed in to face the elements. Just looking at an old picture of my sister and me that winter gives me a claustrophobic feeling. I was so covered up in a one-piece, several-inches-thick, parade-float-looking suit, that rapid movement would have been impossible.

As I got older and wanted to play in the snow with friends, I had to wear those attractive, oversized galoshes secured by metallic clasps. They went on over your regular shoes and made running a challenge. My mother would insist that I wear long johns under my denim jeans, which were usually tucked inside my boots. I also was required to wear a couple of pairs of wool socks, a sweatshirt of some kind, an optional hideously-colored scarf, a jacket with snap buttons, and most times the very

The author, a few months old, is pictured with his sister Beth in the winter of 1947.

From the Jan. 8, 1960, Nashville Banner: "FUN IN THE SNOW—Dwight Williams, son of Mr. and Mrs. S. M. Williams; Bill Shell and Pete Shell, sons of Mr. and Mrs. William A. Shell, play in the deepest snow they have ever seen." (Nashville Public Library, Nashville Room, photo by Jack Gunter)

appealing, fuzzy earmuffs. Those muffs were attached by a couple of thin-metal head bands and adjusted by pulling, or pushing, them together, depending on the size of your noggin. The band went over your head and was covered by a stocking cap or hat of the day. The gloves I wore never seemed to protect against wetness and were always a size too large. All together it made for quite the look. It mattered not, for I fit in with all the other neighborhood kids of that generation. We all were snow-worthy even if we couldn't move.

Snowfalls of five inches or more were regular occurrences during my youth. In addition to the Blizzard of '51 (see page 78) there were many other exciting snow events all through my elementary and high-school years. I was 9 on Jan. 23, 1956, when a snow came so fast you could hardly see. We had five inches in five hours, and schools were closed for three days. Watching weatherman Dr. Carl Seyfert announce on WSM-TV Channel 4 that "schools will be closed" sent all of us into a frenzy. We loved it; our parents…not so much.

The next several winters were great. From 1959 to 1965 Nashville had over 100 inches of snow, most of it coming during school days. In 1960 an all-time record of 38.5 inches fell in the first three months of the year. Wow!

It did not take much to excite us little tots. Our parents and/or siblings would usually pull us down small slopes, icy side roads, or in our front yards, to give us a thrill. Across the street from me, Alex's infamous front-yard hill was often used for a quick rush. It was only 15 to 20 feet long, but a snow slide down it was all a little fellow needed. Alex's dad spent the better part of his life trying to keep us off of it, to no avail.

As I got older, I was allowed to venture out with friends. One of the first such excursions was probably during the snow in 1956. Pulling my hand-me-down American Flyer, with my dog close behind, I met friends on the hill at the far end of Cantrell Avenue, where it seemed hundreds of kids had gathered. After negotiating many trips up and down, we migrated across from Woodmont School to the steep hill at Wilson Boulevard where the older crowd was. That hill was fast and somewhat intimidating to us.

In later years, I moved to more challenging locations. In my mind I had become a veteran sledder, even carrying a used bar of Camay or Lifebuoy soap with me to grease my sled rails for optimum speed. One of those challenging spots was about a half-mile away, across Woodmont Boulevard. They called it the "Big Hill" (not to be mistaken for the "Big Dipper" on Sterling Drive). It was an exceptionally-steep road called Wimbledon. Houses lined either side as it looped from Woodmont and passed by Hilldale, Scarsdale, Ruland, Grayswood, and Foxhall roads before dead-ending after a quarter-mile or so. The crest was right around Scarsdale Drive, where my friend Joel lived. After approximately 30 feet of a very slight decline, the Big Hill dropped dramatically, so much so that it was

From the Jan. 8, 1960, Nashville Banner: "SNOW-MAN—*Drew Shillinglaw and Sunny Shillinglaw, children of Mr. and Mrs. Richard P. Shillinglaw, build a snowman in the yard at their home on Westover Drive.*" (Nashville Public Library, Nashville Room, photo by Jack Gunter)

virtually impossible to come to a stop until one had passed by both Ruland and Grayswood, unless there was a mishap, of course. There were plenty of those.

To make sure the road stayed as treacherous as possible, any car, mail van or delivery vehicle was often hit with snowballs to discourage them from blemishing the venue.

Charlie Bryan, whose home bordered the Big Hill, surmised that if the streets remained snow-covered then another day out of school would be forthcoming. With that in mind, not only Wimbledon needed to remain slick but the heavily-traveled Woodmont Boulevard, as well. Back then vehicles would improve traction by having snow chains put on the tires by neighborhood service stations. The chains would eat up snow-covered streets, and therefore weren't conducive to keeping them pristine for sledding. You could always hear them coming, as they made a clinking, crunching sound. Knowing what destruction chains could do, Charlie and his buddies made snowballs, up to four feet high, and rolled them out on Woodmont to impede

From the Jan. 8, 1960, Nashville Banner: "ONE HORSE SLEIGH—Ann Kerrigan, daughter of Mrs. Phillip Kerrigan, Jr., hitches the pony to the sleigh to pull her brother, Philip Kerrigan, III, and Anne Howe Billings, daughter of Dr. and Mrs. Frederic T. Billings." (Nashville Public Library, Nashville Room, photo by Jack Gunter)

traffic. I applauded the noble effort, but, I am told, it had little impact on school closings.

Back at the hill, "trains" would be assembled. A train was three or more sleds, usually eight to 10, with at least two to three kids on each sled, lined up one behind the other. The galoshes of the kid lying down on the sled in front of you would be hooked into the open steering area at the front of your sled, and so on down the line. When the final sled was hooked onto the end of the train, off all would go, slowly at first, then gradually picking up speed. The leader, by just a slight turn of his sled, would cause a whip effect, exaggerating the turn for the last in line. Those at the rear would end up going sideways at breakneck speeds. Rarely do I remember the last few sleds getting safely to the bottom of the hill. The youngest sledders, totally unaware of what being last in line meant, were often relegated to that spot on the train. Mailboxes, fences, ditches and even animals were caught up in the derailments.

Young Charlie remembers challenging the Beatty's split-rail fence on one trip ("I was unable to walk for days," he recalled). He and brother Allen also took many rides, with up to 15 youngsters, in an old bobsled given to them by their Aunt Nell and Uncle Stewart. That all ended one snowy day when a nosedive into the Beatty's ditch broke it into pieces. All the kids were left intact, and the Beatty family yard became a memorable piece of sledding history.

While at the summit of Wimbledon, we warmed up by the fire set in the Bryan's driveway and waited our turn to go down—single sleds this time. Friend Paul Clements decided to steer, so I lay on top of him. Quite a compromising position, I know, but he was bigger and it was his sled. Hitting warp speed soon after launch, his driving skills eroded quickly, and we veered off the road, barely missing a family pet and some kids walking back up for another run. We careened through a snow-filled culvert and collided with a flimsy sled being pulled by a little girl from the Cockrell family, almost severing it in half. Being chastised by a little girl almost in tears was humbling. I can still hear "You broke Van Leer's sled!" Paul's sled had a metal piece across the front—no match for little Van Leer's ride. We gathered ourselves, pulled our caps down and disappeared among the many other kids dotting the snowscape. Compensating a young child for bisecting her sled wasn't going to happen.

Just behind the houses bordering that site were the long, highly-elevated back yards of Gilbert Smith and Mrs. Grieves. Apparently, the older kids would hose down the grass and make ice ways through the trees. It took some skill to evade the many saplings that led to Sugartree Creek. No way Paul would steer me there. The long walk back to the top through snow-covered grass took its toll on the stamina.

Another mile or so to the southwest, across Hobbs Road to the top of a hill, was the dead-end street of La Vista Drive. Kenny Diehl remembers greasing his sled with a candle from his parent's home and shooting down La Vista onto Trimble Road. He said that if the conditions were right and traffic was blocked, one could make it almost a quarter-mile past Lindawood, Wallace and Sneed to where it intersected with Estes. It was one heck of a ride, and one heck of a walk back.

Any steep hill, road or golf course provided great thrills. Woodmont Country Club was no exception. Sledding there was hazardous for a couple of reasons. First, the management would patrol and run you off, threatening to phone your parents. Secondly, there were steep hills and golf-cart bridges that crossed the west part of Sugartree Creek, adding to the risk. According to Bryan, pal Billy Cunningham once blistered it down a snow-covered fairway, missed the bridge crossing entirely, and ended up in the icy waters. Sitting in a babbling brook at 15 degrees is not what he had envisioned.

That course was seven or eight blocks from my home. I went there once, just as the mercury seemed to bottom out. Survival instincts kicked in, and I made a beeline back to the house with little or no feeling in my blue fingers. My parents, recognizing early frostbite signs when I took off my gloves, advised me to stick them under cold water for a slow thaw. A time-tested remedy. Not heeding their instructions, as usual, I submerged them in hot water instead, to quicken the process. It was a big mistake. My appendages felt like they were going to explode. I let out a few cries, sending my dog Chris scampering out of the room. I learned the hard way.

At grammar school there was no controlling us kids when flakes began to fall. Woodmont had plenty of windows, so there was no concealing what was happening outside. Our teachers were put to the test when snow was in the air, much like what happened when snow began falling on Thursday,

From the Jan. 8, 1960, Nashville Banner: "SNOW HOLIDAY—Ann Williams, daughter of Mr. and Mrs. Louis Williams, III; Linda Carmichael, daughter of Mr. and Mrs. Nelson Carmichael; Peggy White, daughter of John W. White; Patsy Page and Jay Page, children of Mr. and Mrs. J. G. Page, take advantage of the school holiday to go sleigh riding." *(Nashville Public Library, Nashville Room, photo by Jack Gunter)*

Jan. 7, 1960. Only this time we were in a bus, and I was a seventh-grader at Battle Ground Academy in Franklin. I am proud to say my fellow classmates and I survived the longest 20-mile ride to Nashville in history: seven hours. My sub-freshman basketball coach and teacher, Johnny Bennett, was at the wheel. A harrowing experience for him, no doubt, trying to negotiate two-lane Hillsboro Road with a busload of excited boys raising and lowering the windows to let the blowing snow come in. The fishtailing felt like a ride at Fair Park. Coach Bennett was red-faced most of the time and probably had a nip or two after that day ended. Come to think of it, he might have had some wintry cheer along the route as well.

Snow piled up in bunches. We were witnessing the biggest snow in a decade. The snowball fights that subsequently erupted were always fun, especially if you had a good throwing arm. Kids who were most vulnerable always got the worst of it. The "Rounabout Town Campus Chatter" column in the Jan. 8, 1960, Nashville Banner stated, "Snow came to campus (Vanderbilt/Peabody)…and it furnished the main entertainment of the week…there was

In January 1960, friends of the author built a snow fort in the front yard of John Woods. Left to right are: Paul Clements, Livingston Kelley, Phillip Woods, John Woods, Ricky Chambers and a boy believed to be Richard Woods. Another fort had walls over six feet tall.

more than enough snow on 24th Avenue to furnish raw material for snowballs." Snowball fights generally were okay unless you got hit with an especially hard one. Cries of "He's got ice in his!" quickly made the rounds. That was a definite no-no. Those big snows and accompanying snowball fights lent themselves to the construction of snowmen and other unidentifiable objects all over town.

Over on Clearview Drive, Livingston Kelly orchestrated the construction of two substantial snow forts with the help of John Woods and Paul Clements (see photo above). You could launch white missiles at unsuspecting kids and be protected from assault from all comers in those things. One of them had several rooms and another was over six feet tall. They were pieces of amazing winter architecture.

The next month, on Feb. 13, the headline on the Banner stated, "Snow May Reach 8 Inches." In fact, 15 more inches fell in that month. The Crescent Theater on Church, feeling the pinch of sagging attendance, offered a 35-cent Saturday matinee featuring Vincent Price in "The Tingler." It worked on me; I went to see the lobster-like creature roam the aisles.

There was no let up through the 1960s. We got 18 inches on the New

Years Eve of '63 and into January 1964 (see "Late December Back in '63" in the book "When I Was a Kid"). Watauga Lake, in Centennial Park, froze over during December, as temperatures dropped to six degrees. Several of us went there and engaged in a game of soccer/ice hockey with some unknown kids. Goals were set up and anything that would roll or slide became the puck. There were no sticks; kicking was how you scored. All I can remember is that poor Paul kept falling and striking the back of his head on the ice. (Later I figured that must be the reason for his abnormal behavior.)

At that same time, Skyline Drive kids Kenny Diehl and brother Robert pulled their sleds, along with Steve Murray and a buddy called Stoney, to the hilly Murray front yard behind Julia Green Elementary School. They boarded their American Flyers and sped down toward Wallace Road some 50 feet below. Problem was that a tributary of Sugartree Creek was at the bottom of the yard. Good thing it had frozen over.

"You could hit that creek, turn right and almost make it to Abbott Martin Road," recalled Kenny. That must have been quite a ride.

From the Jan. 8, 1960, Nashville Banner: "SNOW ENTHUSIASTS—*Casey Reed, Mac Reed, and Jim Reed, IV, children of Mr. and Mrs. Jim Reed, III, spend the day throwing snowballs and playing in the snow in their yard on Belle Meade Boulevard.*" (Nashville Public Library, Nashville Room, photo by Jack Gunter)

My high-school years were filled with sledding. From Holly Tree Gap down the hill, all the way to Franklin Road, to neighborhood hills and roads, and in particular off Chickering Road and in Percy Warner Park. From December 1967 through March 1968 we had 27 inches of snow. In the midst of this Sam Herbert, David Proctor, and some Vanderbilt fraternity brothers found the hood of an old Plymouth in the woods overlooking the Steeplechase site in the park. It was one of those with the bullet type nose. After dragging it out of the snow-covered thicket, they realized that five or six people could get on and use it like a bobsled. With the aid of some brandy, a good time was had, and everyone survived. No word on the Plymouth hood, or how it even got there.

My carefree sledding days basically ended by 1971, with the birth of my first child. From those very early years throughout the 1950s and '60s, it was a great time to be a kid and to frolic in those winter wonderlands. Bundling up and sledding down those treacherous slopes, and warming up by outside fires, were rites of passage, you might say. I almost miss those fuzzy earmuffs and cumbersome galoshes…almost.

CHAPTER 2

Scouting Days

REALIZING HIS men had no idea how to survive in the wilderness, a British Army officer named Robert Stephenson Smyth Baden-Powell wrote a little handbook, around the end of the 19th century, called "Aids to Scouting," emphasizing adaptability and frontier skills. He had small packs with a single leader and gave badges out for exemplary service. He later took 20 boys to Brownsea Island, off the coast of England, for 12 days to see how his handbook, and implementations within it, would work with kids; it was a rousing success. The next year, in 1908, he published "Scouting for Boys." His system flourished overseas. It took Chicago businessman William Boyce getting lost in England's fog to get America going. After a youngster directed him out of the haze of the city, Boyce offered to tip him, but the kid refused, stating he was a Boy Scout and could not take a tip for a good turn. Boyce was intrigued,

The cover for the 1955 Cub Scout Christmas catalog. (Artfire)

The author was in Cub Scout Den 4 at Woodmont School in 1955. Back row (left to right): Alex Slabosky, Michael Dorman, Jimmy Goode, Johnny Felts and Den Mother Molly Slabosky. Front row: the author, Ralph Keller, Pat Davy and Barry Levine.

gathered information about these scouts, and on Feb. 8, 1910, incorporated the Boy Scouts of America.

Cub Scouting came later—it was formally launched in 1930. Dens met weekly at members' homes, where crafts, games, and ceremonies were enjoyed by the Scouts. Packs met weekly or semi-monthly, with competitions between dens being the focus. The original badges—among them Bobcat, Wolf (age 9), Bear (age 10), and Lion (age 11)—took their names from Kipling's "The Jungle Book." The Webelos designation appeared in 1954. Akela, Den and Pack all came from that classic.

Steve Power recalls receiving his Wolf badge at Julia Green School around 1955–1956, from Los Angeles Ram quarterback (and former Vandy and Woodmont School kid) Bill Wade. It was a huge event for those boys.

When I came along in the 1950s, to be a Cub Scout you had to be between the ages of 7 and 10, or from the first through the fifth grades. I was encouraged to participate after my second grade at Woodmont, for, as I recall, some outside regimentation was needed. Most every grade school was associated with scouting back then. Woodmont even had Brownie and Cub Scout troop leaders in all the pertinent grades. Scout membership nationwide went from 2.8 million to 5.2 million during the 1950s.

I thought this whole scouting thing was kind of neat at first, because we got some colorful uniforms upon which you could have your mom sew badges and pins. We got those neck scarves with that gold thingy through which to thread it, a cap, and a belt with a brass buckle that fastened down on the cloth part. It was kind of like the cavalry soldiers we saw in the Western movies on television and in the theaters. Kids ended up wearing them to school on meeting days and some just played outside with the shirt on just like any other shirt. I am not so sure that was proper Cub Scout etiquette.

Our dens consisted of seven or eight kids, usually supervised by a Den Mother. God bless those mothers. It was not easy at times, particularly trying to corral a bunch of hyperactive boys.

Our meeting always started off by reciting the Cub Scout Promise: "I, (name), Promise To do my Best, To do my Duty, To God and My Country, To be Square, And to obey the Law of the Pack."

The Pack law went like this: "The Cub Scout follows Akela. The Cub Scout helps the pack go. The pack helps the Cub Scout grow. The Cub Scout gives goodwill."

I never knew what Akela was, but have since found out it meant the adult leader. The term "to be square" was changed in 1971 because of the influence of the times, similar to what happened to "gay," a word that in my school books meant "happy." Boy…have things changed.

I was in Den 4 at Woodmont in 1955 under the tutelage of Molly Slabosky (for a while anyway). One of our meetings took place at Rob Skinner's home on Lynbrook Road, just a few houses away from mine. This particular meeting ended up in a near-melee triggered by what I think was too much gulping of Anthony's chocolate milk. As I recall, two of us were to demonstrate, to our fellow Bobcats, the art of the pugil stick or quarterstaff, like Little John used to

The Cub Scout Promise on a plaque circa 1955. (Etsy)

knock Robin Hood off of the bridge. It turns out that Ralph got a little aggressive with me or Barry, causing the classic technique of jousting to turn into a swinging-for-the-head type of motion. Unfortunately, everyone sitting in a circle watching the demonstration had access to one of these implements. It turned into an every-Cub-for-himself situation. Molly and Mrs. Skinner finally restored order by holding up the calming two-fingers and threatening life and limb. If I am not mistaken, the Skinners withdrew their name as revolving den hosts after that. The Law of the Pack went by the wayside that day.

I don't seem to remember the Pinewood Derby, or if I even bothered to enter the races, because you had to build your own entry. Let's just say that my construction skills were inadequate. (The year 1953 was the first time for the Pinewood Derby). Fred Cloud took third place honors for Pack 210 at Crieve Hall School back in 1966 and still has his trophy. I assume Fred could whittle wood, and I'm sure he was applauded for his, or his folks', efforts.

The only applause I remember receiving was at a massive jamboree held at the State Fairgrounds. Thousands of scouts attended with like numbers of proud family members in the stands. Our troop marched into a big arena to continuous applause, for which I remain grateful.

When my "cubbing" days ended, I slowly moved to Boy Scouts. It was a short-lived experience. The only redeeming value I got from it was being influenced by a wonderful man named Asa Scobey Rogers. Here was a man who had cerebral palsy so bad he could not walk until age 11. He went on to get his Eagle Scout badge, and later his engineering degree from Vanderbilt. He invented a machine designed to wrap our beloved Goo Goo candy bars and, I am told, came up with the first letter-sorting

A Cub Scout Den meeting is pictured in 1955 in Winston Salem, N.C. (Boy Scouts Museum)

device used by the United States Post Office. He became Scoutmaster of Troop 9 and founded Troop 121 at Woodmont Baptist Church. That is where I went. He was a special person, but he had his work cut out when I started my Tenderfoot year.

Trying to tie the square knot, the bowline, half stitch, etc., tested my patience, of which I had none. However, I was adept at the granny knot and could comfortably replicate the slip knot. I was also good at a knife game (since discouraged for safety reasons) that we called "Splits" at Camp Boxwell, where hazing rituals, such as blindfolding new scouts and making them walk barefoot across hot coals, was prevalent. The hot coals were just ice, but it felt like the real thing. I might add this was not in the Scout handbook. We also never caught a "snipe," but we darn sure went on many a snipe hunt.

My scouting days finally derailed when, to make the Star designation, I had to learn the Morse Code. At a home on the corner of Lynnwood and Sunnybrook Drive, my test began...and abruptly ended. Those dot... dot... dots... and the dash- dash- dashes, became confused with the dit, dit, dits, and the dah, dah, dahs. I finally turned to the leader and said: "This is the end, end, end, so I will see, see, see ya." I left, never to return.

The girls in grade school had their own scouting system. They started as Brownies, originally called Rosebuds. Folk stories describe Brownies as good-natured spirits, goblins or magical little people who would appear around the home, late at night, and do good deeds. No one ever saw them, only a shadow or two...maybe. Baden-Powell supposedly named them after an 1870 story, "The Brownies," by Juliana Horatia Ewing. Some tales say they used to dance around toadstools, which is why some were placed in the center of a ring at Pack meetings. Legend

The cover of the Fall 1950 "Brownie Scout Equipment" catalog. (Girl Scouts)

Nancy (Egbert) Bedford is seen in full Girl Scout regalia in 1958. She was in Troop 321 at Woodmont School.

does not say if the mushrooms were hallucinogenic.

Clara Lisetor-Lane established the Girl Scouts of America (GSA) in 1911 in Des Moines, Iowa, and Juliette Gordon Low established the Girl Guides at about the same time. Low attempted to join forces with the Campfire Girls (my mother was one), but was rejected, as the Campfire Girls were much bigger. Next she tried to merge with the GSA, but Lisetor-Lane felt she had copycatted her group and threatened to sue. Low had the social backing and Lane did not, leading to the eventual demise of the GSA. Low changed the name of the Girl Guides to the Girl Scouts of the United States of America in 1913, and moved from Savannah, Ga., to Washington, D.C. "Daisy" Low was an avid tennis player, rower and outdoors gal. She loved pets, riding horses, helping others, and standing on her head on her birthday. No word if toadstools played a part in that activity either.

Brownies are the youngest Girl Scouts, followed by Juniors and then Cadettes. Here were the rules for a Brownie in 1955:

—*Are in grades 2–4.*

—*Must attend four meetings before being Invested, where they will wear their uniforms for the first time.*

—*Do not go overnight troop camping.*

—*Do not have a program built on awards; there are no Brownie Try-Its, badges or fun patches.*

—*Leaders plan meetings from activity ideas in the girl's handbook and the leader handbook—a real, hardcover book!*

Intermediates are the girls in green that most folks call "Girl Scouts." Some of the Girl Scout rules that same year::

—*Are in grades 5–8.*

—*Must pass the Tenderfoot Rank requirements before being invested and receiving their Tenderfoot (Girl Scout) pin.*

—*No one wears her uniform until the Investiture Ceremony. (Also called Fly-Ups.)*

—*They must pass the Second Class requirements before they may earn badges.*

—*There are no fun patches and no swaps, except at national and international events.*

—*They camp out in tents, cook over an open fire and "lash" camp furniture, as most sites do not include shelters with picnic tables.*

—*There are no flush toilets or hot-water showers. And no horseback riding, swimming, canoeing, archery, or adventure courses, except at summer camp.*

—*You go troop camping to hike, cook out, and work on badges!*

I'd be flying away, not up. The girls also had a promise and laws similar to what we had as Cubs.

Speaking of camping out, washing hair at Camp Woodhaven in Burns, Tenn., was not an option. You didn't. Mary De (Heckman) Elliston went

A group of girls between Brownie and Girl Scout are pictured at Camp Woodhaven in May 1957. (MaryDe [Heckman] Elliston)

there in May 1957 to commemorate the ending of her Brownie years and the beginning of her Girl Scout career. She was assigned to a tent housing three other scouts. Keeping their quarters neat and clean was of the utmost importance, as required by a daily inspection. The cleanest in camp was given a magnificent trophy, "a beautiful tin can, extra large with coat hanger handles [that were] curved, attached at the top and bottom to make it look like a loving cup." A few years later, at Camp Sycamore in Ashland City, Denise Volz said she contracted poison ivy every spring, plus "ghost stories got everyone spooked at camp." Yvonne Eaves laments: "There should have been a badge for telling Bell Witch stories and snipe hunting."

In 1956, Mary De's Brownie Troop 26 put on a play on Juliette Low Day where most everyone at Julia Green School attended. Invitations were even mailed out to local folks. Bobbie Edmondson Markham was a Brownie at Crieve Hall and got to go on the "Popeye Show" on television with Captain Bob. Now that sounds like fun. At Bellshire Elementary, Libby Parsons was the Brownie leader for Lisa Johnson, who bought her uniform from McClure's, recalling her dad even tied her first tie. Jamie Sharer Smith said their Brownie leader would walk with them from St. Edwards to Coleman Park for meetings. Susan Marshall Kirk's mom, Betsy, led the Brownies and girl scouts at Crieve Hall in the 1950s and '60s, and recalls that one craft project involved melting down old vinyl records. Another project enabled her to earn the roller skate badge at the Thompson Lane Roller Drome. That is one badge I would have earned.

Not all kids have fond memories, kind of like me. For instance, scout camp was not for Kirk, as the odor of dirt and the sight of lizards is

Front cover of a Brownie play invitation that was mailed to folks in February 1956. The play took place at Julia Green School. (MaryDe [Heckman] Elliston)

a memory that haunts her to this day. Her mother had to come and get her four days into a scheduled two-week event. "Not my proudest moment," she admitted. Her idea of camping out now is a hotel with room service. A girl after my own heart. Charles Barbara Lewis had her glasses knocked off at her Brownie troop at Knox School, and when she went to Eakin she was told rudely to "start your own troop." Cliorie Licody Bradley met at Jere Baxter School: "I never think of that troop that I do not think of the other leader. She left town with all of our supplies, even our flag and cash."

Good times far outweighed the negative ones, for as Eaves put it: "I am a better adult because of the influence of Girl Scouting. So many wonderful memories." Brownie Margaret Ann Slaughter had "great memories and a good time at Camp Sycamore raising and lowering the flag, sleeping in tents and doing everything in a group." Mae Hamilton Ambrose's father was a Cub leader and kept the scout flag until his death. Now that is dedication, and it gives one an idea of what a good man he was. Dixie Tanksley was a Brownie leader and a Cub Scout Den Mother, organizing banquets, Christmas parades and overnight camp-outs for years. "I put 20 years into ten," she recalled. "I had over 75 different boys and girls and felt like everyone of them was mine. [They were] some of the happiest days of my life."

Brownies, Cubs, Boy Scouts and Girl Scouts were all based on wholesome qualities, and, at one point, centered around our neighborhood schools and homes. You would be hard pressed to find many neighborhood schools (if there are any) that still provide the foundations we had back during those times. Those Den Mothers, camp counselors, parents, school administrators and dedicated volunteers created great memories and influenced many a young child. We all would be better off if we followed the note found in Baden-Powell's desk after his death in 1941. It read: "Try and leave this world a little better than you found it." That is what Scouting is all about.

CHAPTER 3

In the Mood

THOSE BIG bands of yesteryear had that swinging, happy-go-lucky, melodic, romantic sound that kept kids and adults in the mood for decades. It swept over the nation, eliciting memories of that Flexible Flyer sled, kids staying outside on long summer nights, and dates at the soda fountain. My parents were just college kids in the 1930s, and I feel sure they dropped a nickel or two in the juke box to hear those classics by Glenn Miller, The Dorsey Brothers, Woody Herman, Count Basie, Artie Shaw, Woody Herman, Benny Goodman and the like. The airwaves back then were filled with all those greats.

I heard those sounds in my early youth, as my father had purchased a 10-record LP set entitled "Glenn Miller and His Orchestra—Limited Edition" in 1954. Before rock-and-roll took over, my parents, sisters, and their friends and neighbors, often put those 33 1/3 "non-breakables" over the spindle of our Victrola and took in those wondrous vibes.

Snooky Lanson (left) and Owen Bradley in 1946. (Patsy Bradley)

In 1956, Owen Bradley and Dinah Shore performed together at the Ryman Auditorium for her nationally-telecast "The Dinah Shore Chevy Show." (Patsy Bradley)

Nashville's Francis Craig Orchestra was one of the top attractions for society types, sororities, fraternities and gala club events from the 1930s into the 1940s. His 1947 recording of "Near You" went to No. 1 and was featured on the national telecast of "Your Hit Parade," with host Snooky Lanson. It came as a surprise to him, for his career was winding down at the time. It became Milton Berle's theme song on the "Texaco Star Theatre."

Local orchestras packed in the crowds at the clubs in 1941. There was Phil Harris and his orchestra at the Knickerbocker Theatre. Bob Young and the Billy Shelton orchestras swung away. Fred Shumate graced the Palms on Franklin Road and the White Horse at 220 Meridian Street. Adrian McDowell played the Colonial Dinner Club on Harding Road. The Tommy Knowles Orchestra entertained at the Rock Garden on Dickerson Road and at the Paradise Ballroom at 806 Eighth Avenue North. Ethel Goodman's Hot Shots Orchestra, Horace Henderson's 15-piece swing band, and Jack Dozier and his Harlem Swing Band were also at the Paradise. Paul Carroll and his Southern Colonels played country clubs, fraternity and sorority events. Horace Holley Orchestra, Johnny Sharpe, Neil Owen Band, Jimmy Melton and Horace Heidt's Band were all over town. Jack Yandel's Orchestra often appeared at the Pines and Walter Gammel squeezed the accordion around

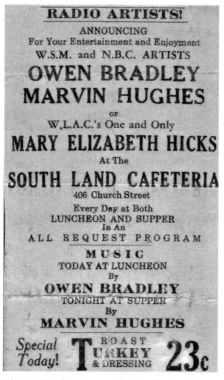

This 1947 advertisement for Bradley's orchestra at the South Land Cafeteria appeared in the Nashville Banner. (Patsy Bradley)

town for select groups. The movie "Sun Valley Serenade," with Glenn Miller and his orchestra played at the Belle Meade Theatre. It was the beginning of the "war years" and Big Band was going strong.

Fourteen years prior, in 1927, a 12-year-old boy who had moved to Nashville from a farm in Westmoreland at age 7, was hit in the eye with a mud ball thrown by a fellow Glenn Elementary classmate. That slinger of the mud is not known, but the kid who got hit became a super star in the music industry. His name was Owen Bradley. Getting pegged in the eye and injured for six months is no fun, but, according to younger brother Harold, it enabled young Owen to learn to play by ear the Hawaiian guitar and master the ivories on the family player piano that he foot-pumped in his home on Lucille Street.

Bradley's real foray into the music world started after the eighth grade at age 15. His dad made him choose between going to work or going to school. Bradley considered music fun, so the choice was simple. The piano became the tool of his trade, and he played all over town whenever he could find work.

Eventually his reputation as an accomplished pianist began to take hold. One of his big breaks came when he played at the Hippodrome Walkathon in 1934. These Depression-Era events featured pairs of walkers and dancers in an endurance competition for hundreds of dollars, complete with live bands, an audience, and a comedic master of ceremonies. Some of these were broadcast on WLAC radio. It was a big deal and took place in cities across the country.

Young Bradley played piano at the Walkathon with Buddy Hubbard and His Boys during the midnight hour in February of that year. The emcee was famed nightclub comic, former Nashvillian and first cousin to Dinah Shore, Harry Jarkey. In June he recommended Bradley to the walkathon manager in Roanoke, Va. A Western Union Telegram arrived offering Bradley work in a band to perform in Norfolk and in Wheeling, W. Va., for $22 per week, with board no less. It was just one of many such offers he received.

Bradley took gigs with many bands in all kind of establishments. He played at The Merry-Garden and Silver Slipper Beer Garden on Gallatin Road, the Pines and the Ridgeway Inn out on Harding, Hettie Rays' atop Nine Mile Hill, the Stork Club on Franklin Road, and numerous gambling halls, and in other counties as well. Back then some supper clubs had a cover charge of 55 cents, others nothing. Bradley performed at South Land Cafeteria during a roast-turkey-and-dressing dinner that cost 23 cents. What a deal.

There was even romance for Bradley. His grade-school sweetheart, Mary Katherine Franklin, followed his performances from the earliest days, even

Owen Bradley (at piano) and his orchestra at the Hermitage Hotel circa 1946. Singer Snooky Lanson is on the far right. Others are: Ted Swiney, bass; Harold Bradley, guitar; Augie Clemenger, saxophone; Charlie Grant, saxophone; Dutch McMillan, saxophone; Paul (last name unknown), saxophone; Gish Gilbertson, saxophone; Walter Link, drums; Bill McElhiney, trumpet; Carl Garvin, trumpet; (unidentified), trumpet; Jim Hall, trumpet; Scobey Dill, trombone; and Young Harper, trombone. (Patsy Bradley)

In 1943, Owen Bradley performed with Bing Crosby at the Belle Meade Country Club to raise money for war bonds. Left to right: Jack Shook (with guitar, cropped), Beasley Smith, George Cooper (with bass behind Bing Crosby), Bing Crosby, Kay Armen, Owen Bradley (at piano), and Farris Coursey (on drums). (Patsy Bradley, photo by John E. Hood)

writing in her scrapbook over an advertisement for a Ridgeway Inn show: "What a place, and the piano player, Oh Boy!" They married on Dec. 14, 1935. She became the supportive backbone of the family.

By 1940 he had tickled the ivories with The Happiness Boys Orchestra, Ted Swinney, Red McEwen, Charles Nagy, Carl Garvin and Beesley Smith. When in the U.S. Merchant Marines he played in the Ted Weems Service Band, and in 1942 accompanied crooner Bing Crosby at the Belle Meade Country Club to raise war bonds. That same year he, Beesley Smith and Marvin Hughes wrote the hit "Night Train To Memphis" for Roy Acuff. His dedication to relentlessly practicing paid off, for he became known all over town as the "Prince of the Ivories."

He eventually put together his own dance band and was named music director for WSM, where he had started out as a "spot" man in 1935. In 1946, using the name Brad Brady and His Tennesseans, he recorded "Zeb's Mountain Boogie" on Bullet Records and sold 75,000 copies. In 1947 his Owen Bradley

Orchestra performed live radiocasts, such as "Lion Oil Presents Sunday Down South," "Morton Salt Show," "Noontime Neighbors," and "The Waking Crew." Most were broadcast in front of audiences at the National Life and Accident Insurance Company building.

Daughter Patsy said she, her mom, and brother Jerry were often in the crowd at the "Sunday Down South" show. "It was quite a deal," she said.

That orchestra consisted of 12 to 15 pieces, and included brother Harold, who played guitar. Show vocalists included Bob Johnstone, Buddy Hall, Kitty Kallen, Kay Carlisle, Delores Watson and Dottie Dillard, who would soon join The Anita Kerr Singers. Snooky Lanson was the vocalist in the orchestra and went on to become a star on NBC-TV's "Your Hit Parade" and later a deejay at WAMB.

Bradley's orchestra became the premier dance band for sorority, fraternity, bachelor club, country club and society events all across town. They played the Big Band favorites at Colmere Club, Cotillion Club, Sewanee, Columbia Military Academy, Castle Heights, Steeplechase parties, Dunbar Cave resort and "Furbelows and Fanfare."

Bradley signed with Coral Records in 1949, and in 1950 he was the musical arranger and piano player with Red Foley on the recording of "Chattanoogie Shoe Shine Boy" at Castle Studio in the Tulane Hotel. It was No. 1 for 13 weeks. He also learned a lot from the head of Decca Records, Paul Cohen, with whom he was an apprentice at that time.

Bradley's unique ability to remember the patrons and their favorite songs was amazing. Recognizing a familiar face in the crowd, the band would break into the tune, stunning the guest and further enamoring the audience. The orchestra was a regular at the Hermitage Hotel and the Colonial Ballroom at the downtown Maxwell House Hotel, serenading high school and college kids. The Maxwell House was surrounded by beautiful, white, Corinthian-style columns. There were arched doors and windows bordering the dance floor, and there was a fireplace bordered by mirrors on each side.

Young Patsy was just the right age to attend such galas in the 1950s. As she put it: "I was the most-chaperoned kid in town." Her father's orchestra put everyone in the mood, as she and her date would say hello to the band members, speak to her dad and proceed to another part of the room. Most of her dates never knew she was his daughter until she spoke to him. Brother Jerry (while not drag racing on "the boulevard") often attended, once giving a boy $5 to dance with her. Patsy was appalled. As pretty as she was, it would not have taken any arm-twisting to get a dance partner. (Sorry I wasn't there, for I would have paid Jerry myself.)

Transporting and setting up all of the orchestra equipment was no small task. That was assigned to "band boys" like Wilson Horde. At one performance, the elevators at the Maxwell House would not hold the organ and piano. Ever resourceful, he solicited some bellhops to help carry the instruments to the second-floor mezzanine overlooking the lobby. Guess that labor came out of the night's proceeds.

Another event there caused some panic but was calmed by Bradley's demeanor and quick thinking. In April 1955, during the Delta Sigma high-school fraternity spring dance, the kitchen behind the ballroom caught fire. Patsy recalls: "As smoke filled the room the orchestra broke into 'Smoke Gets in Your Eyes' as everyone calmly exited." Just five years later, on Christmas

A 1947 performance on "Lion Oil Presents Sunday Down South." Owen Bradley is conducting (back to the camera). (Patsy Bradley)

A 1947 advertisement for "Owen Bradley and His N.B.C. Orchestra." (Patsy Bradley)

Day 1961, the Maxwell House burned down.

Back in those days, there were "no-break" songs given to the band, songs during which the tapping on the shoulder to break into a dance with someone else's partner was not allowed. They were usually tunes towards the end of the evening and were the type that facilitated getting cuddly with your date. Those given to the band on the night of April 30, 1950, were some classics: "Blue Moon," "Embraceable You," "Night and Day," "Stardust," "Always," "Time on my Hands" and "Nightie Night." Bradley's Orchestra always ended the dances with a mood-enhancing medley of "The Party's Over," "For All We Know," "I'll See You in my Dreams" and "Goodnight Sweetheart." A closing like that would require close chaperoning for the rest of the evening.

Owen and Harold built two film studios over the years. The first in 1951 was designed for short music films. Originally located at Second and Lindsey, it was later moved across the alley from Woolworth's off 21st in Hillsboro Village. Here they made Army and Air Force recruitment films with country music stars. Patsy recalls they once needed an audience, so she and Jerry were asked to bring their classmates to applaud and laugh. Each kid got from 50 cents to $1. Guess the louder you laughed the more you were paid.

In 1954 they bought a house at 804 16th Ave. S. for $7,500 and added an Army Quonset Hut for another $7,500. Opening in 1955, it was called Bradley Film and Recording Studios. Bradley's hit "White Silver Sands" (1957) and the Duane Eddy-style instrumental "Big Guitar" (Owen Bradley

Quintet, 1958) were both recorded there. The hut was sold to Columbia Records in 1962. In 1964 Owen converted an old barn in Mt. Juliet into a demo studio for son Jerry to learn the trade.

In December 1964, while I was enjoying high-school basketball, going to combos, and listening to such refined tunes as "Little GTO" and "The Jerk," the Owen Bradley Orchestra was playing its "Last Dance" at Hillwood Country Club. The show was recorded specifically "For band members, their families and friends only." A warning on the album stated: "Persons under 55 may experience nausea!!!" For all practical purposes that was Nashville's last great Big-Band performance by an orchestra that was actually around during those swinging and jitterbugging years.

Hall-of-Fame honors, producing and recording for his "angels" (Patsy Cline, Brenda Lee, Loretta Lynn, Kitty Wells, k.d. lang, and many others), a bronze statue, album-of-the-year awards, leader of Nashville's last great, authentic Big Band, etc., etc., do not eclipse the honesty, humbleness and integrity that characterized the man. As daughter Patsy stated, "His personality left almost as lasting a legacy as his music."

Thousands of fans, kids and party-goers who were put "in the mood" by the Owen Bradley Orchestra across the decades were fortunate souls. I only wish I would have been there, too.

CHAPTER 4

Halloween 1959

WHERE DID all this tricking, treating, dressing up and pumpkin carving come from? Some say it was a Celtic tradition at the end of each year, when the dead and the living overlapped and demons would roam about. Dressing up as those spirits of the dead may have become a custom. Others say that back in the ninth century in Europe, "souling" would take place on Nov. 2, on what was called All Souls Day. The less fortunate would beg for "soul cakes" at the homes of the wealthy. The more soul cakes one received, the more prayers would be said for dead relatives, thereby hastening their passage to heaven.

It is widely believed that the Scottish brought trick-or-treating, or "guising" as they called it, to America in the 19th century. It was nothing more than putting on a costume, singing a rhyme, doing a card trick or telling a story in exchange for a treat. I am part Scottish, and I never sang or did card tricks for treats. However, I did tell some stories, for

This Halloween-themed Brach's Candy ad appeared in the October 1959 issue of LIFE magazine.

which I was often punished.

As far as pumpkins go, since the 16th century, a British boy was known as a "jack." A "jack," who was a night watchman and thus carried a lantern, was the basis of the term "jack-o-lantern." During times of fog and heavy mist over bogs and wetlands, there would appear strange lights, said to be fairies and ghosts. Pranksters, usually young boys, would hollow out gourds (later pumpkins), place candles inside, and then hide in these poorly-visible swamps while swinging the gourds, thereby spooking citizens into believing specters were hanging out on the moors. Those ghostly-lit heads became lore.

In America, by the 1920s, pranks had become the Halloween activity of choice, which was only made worse by the Great Depression. That activity led to an organized effort to tame vandalism in our communities and to make trick-or-treating a highly-supervised tradition by the 1930s. Before the 1940s, most Americans were unfamiliar with the term "trick-or-treat," and what there was of it diminished greatly during WWII, as sugar-rationing curtailed candy production. Post-war "Baby Boomers" reclaimed the tradition of trick-or-treating in the 1950s, and newly-built suburbs fueled the resurrection.

"The Giant Gila Monster" (1959) (impawards.com)

Putting on a costume was a big thing for us little ones in the early 1950s. We could pretend to be whatever or whomever we wanted to be, dressing up as a cowboy, Donald Duck, a space ranger, a nursery-rhyme character, a Wizard of Oz character, a clown, vampire, wolf man, glow-in-the-dark skeleton or Casper the Friendly Ghost (just throw a sheet with eye holes over your head and that was it). Those Halloweens consisted of several of us neighborhood kids gathering at a home or meeting out on the street after dark with our paper sacks, then heading out to canvass all houses within walking distance. After several hours of unsupervised walking and ringing doorbells (parents just let us roam by ourselves back then), we usually congregated back at my place, where Mom had a big punch bowl of "something" in the middle of our dining room table. There we dumped out the goodies to see what we had received. It was a big event.

By 1959, at age 12, I only put on a black bandit mask and ball cap. Frightening. It did qualify as a costume and allowed me to continue to acquire—if only for one more year—a lot of goodies, such as candy corn, Sugar Daddy's, Dubble Bubble gum, Pops Rite popcorn, Brach's Candies, candy bars, apples, oranges, unwrapped homemade stuff and even small chess pies. Really bad tasting items, dates and stuff like that, ended up in boxwoods or being used as edible projectiles hurled at younger goblins.

The scare in later years of razor blades and needles hidden in our candy was unheard of then. Those exaggerated myths all began in 1959, when a deranged California dentist gave out laxatives disguised as treats. He was charged with "outrage of public decency." I suppose that phrase stemmed from a child's reaction a few minutes after consumption. A masquerading Cinderella, after eating such stuff, would have sensed a spell coming on her long before the 12 o'clock hour.

Advertisements were bountiful as usual that year. A number of those were intended to make us believe their product was made especially for Halloween, whether it made sense or not. The October issues of LIFE magazine featured a Kool-Aid pitcher looking like a pumpkin, and another featured three ghosts holding a triple pack of Post cereal. Our local Jersey Farms Milk Company ran a huge ad in the Nashville Banner called "Goblin Good...Bring on the Cats, Bats and Pointed Hats." To me Halloween doesn't come to mind when I think of milk and cereal.

Esso gas stations featured a large cartoon jack-o-lantern offering half-priced trick-or-treat candies with the purchase of gasoline. The thought of gasoline candy doesn't fire up the taste buds either. Even better was this one

32 Best of Times

Above is part of a Woolworth's advertisement that appeared in the Oct. 22, 1959, Nashville Banner. *(Tennessee State Library and Archives)*

on Oct. 30: "Look Kids! Double Treat, Free Halloween Mask with each pound of Smith My Boy Wieners." I guess you could wear the mask, whatever it was, and then have your mom give out the wieners as treats to all the kiddos who came by. I can't think of anything more exciting than saying "trick or treat" and then getting a floppy hot dog put in your bag. Mm, Mmmm!

Woolworth's sold the "newest costumes and masks—Mickey Mouse, Donald Duck, Sleeping Beauty, Tweety, Devil, Witch, Black Cat and Pirate…Child sizes $1.49." (Wonder what the adult-sized Tweety cost?) A kid's rubber mask was only 29 cents while the adult sizes were 39 cents. The ad did not say what the mask looked like.

Grants sold "complete costumes" for $1.98, and "more exciting ones" for $2.98. Who knows what that meant, but it was comforting to know that "All are Flameproof." Thank goodness for that. Every parent was concerned about someone creeping up behind their little Timmy and trying to blow torch his Bozo costume. Now there were no worries.

Not to be outdone, Walgreen's costumes ran $1.33, ages 4 to 14, stating: "All Rayon—in Gay or Scary Styles with Matching Mask." To me, there was no better way to trick-or-treat than to wear an all-rayon costume with a gay, matching mask. I passed on that ensemble.

Ever since Ken Bramming's "Shock Theater" came on Channel 8, I had become a fan of horror films and had even purchased some 45-rpm records down at Buckley's Record Shop on Church Street that were fright related. One was "Frankenstein of '59," by Buchanan and Goodman. "Dinner with Drac," by Zacherle, the Cool Ghoul, recorded in 1958, I happened to win in a "Name it and Claim It" contest from Lee Dorman's neighborhood radio station just a few houses away.

As an alternative to the macabre movies in theaters that October, the teen heartthrob Fabian and sexy Carol Lynley appeared in "Hound Dog Man" on Halloween night at the Paramount (featuring Dodi Stevens singing "Pink Shoe Laces"). From what I was told, that cinema treasure should have been classified as a horror film.

Just down the street at the Tennessee Theater, the science-fiction dazzler "4-D MAN" played to a different bunch of kids. Enticing folks to see that one, Jack Harris, the producer, offered $1,000,000 to anyone who could duplicate what the 4-D Man did in the movie. If you thought you could, the newspaper ad said "Get forms and details at the theater." I didn't see it, so I had no clue as to what he did, but I saw Edward throw up at flute practice once in grade school, and the remnants of his salmon croquet passed over several heads. I should have picked up some forms.

Most of these horror films surrounding Halloween of 1959 catered to the high-school crowd and varied according to content. These, most of which I saw, included: "House on Haunted Hill," with Vincent Price;

"Curse of the Undead" (1959) (impawards.com)

"Hound of the Baskervilles," with two of my favorite actors, Peter Cushing and Christopher Lee; "The Tingler," with Price again; "The Mummy," also starring Cushing and Lee; "The Bat," with Price yet again; "Attack of the Giant Leeches"; "Plan 9 From Outer Space"; "The Giant Gila Monster"; "The Killer Shrews"; "The Hideous Sun Demon"; "The Angry Red Planet"; "Teenagers from Outer Space" and "Teenage Zombies" (seems those delinquent teens were always way out).

On that Halloween night, the Inglewood Theater doubled up with "The Mummy" and "The Curse of the Undead," stating they were suitable "For Teens and Adults." Being only 12 and not of driving age, I missed out on having a terrified young lass jump into my lap at the Bel Air Drive-in on Charlotte when the triple-feature billed as "Bloody Halloween, Weak Hearts Beware, Special Halloween Spook-a-Thon" was offered up. Scaring teens that night was "Horror of Dracula" ("Chilling," the management said), "The Thing That Couldn't Die," followed by "Monster From Green Hell." Further enticing teen fright fanatics, the ad in the paper read, "Can Your Heart Stand the Horror?" followed by the sinister "Warning, Our insurance does not cover death by fright." I suppose that was to keep those stodgy old folks away.

Mischief seemed to be part of that Halloween just like others before it. It was a rainy Saturday night in 1959 and with it came a weatherman's alert in The Nashville Tennessean: "Witches are

"House on Haunted Hill" (1959) (impawards.com)

advised to leave off heavy coats but brooms should be equipped with water wings for successful flying."

Barbasol shave cream proved to be particularly efficient in its sticking power to windshields, hood ornaments and leather car seats, even in wet conditions. I also recollect the plight of an unfortunate citizen, on Kenner Avenue, who happened to leave his "hose pipe" connected to the water hydrant in his front yard. Some goblins, up to no good, dragged the hose pipe up to the house, braced it between the screen door and the front door, turned on the spicket full blast, rang the bell and scampered off into the darkness.

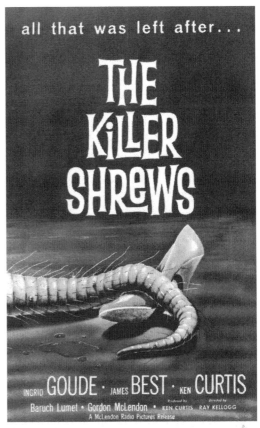

"The Killer Shrews" (1959) (impawards.com)

When the door was opened...well, one can imagine. The door slammed shut but quickly reopened. There appeared a drenched, flashlight-bearing individual, wearing a house coat and slippers, spouting vulgarities, who ran all the way down to the hydrant to turn off the water. He then illuminated nearby shrubs, trees and adjacent yards, determined to find the tricksters, but to no avail.

That same night my fellow spooks and I became the target of a bunch of hoods slinging eggs from their souped-up, muffler-less auto. Maybe one or two hit John and me, but we avoided the other ones as the juvenile delinquents roared past us. From then on, any headlights we saw headed our way caused a mad dash for cover. Years later, having drawn on this experience, we continued that time-honored tradition.

A statement by John Sullivan, dispatcher of the Belle Meade Police in October 1959, put "tricking" this way: "The older ones go out and really trick. They steal house signs and pull posts out of the ground. When a sign is planted in concrete and is uprooted, we know little kids didn't do it." No kidding, John. "Halloween is a safe outing, which doesn't necessarily imply destruction." "Necessarily" being the key word.

Pediatrician Sam W. Carney explained his theory of kids and Halloween in The Nashville Tennessean: "Small children are fascinated by masks. It mostly appeals to the 4-10 year old age group, after that they get too old for it. It gives a good release from pent-up emotions. They need a chance to blow off some steam." I can still hear it now: "Gee, Mom, I had so much pent-up emotion that I decided to blow off steam by writing scary things with a bar of Lux soap on Mr. _____'s car. "

All that being said, it was probably my last night to go spooking. Now a sub-freshman in a different school, I moved on to another youthful phase. Trick-or-treating and pretending I was who-knows-what became part of the past, just like all the ghosts and goblins that had roamed my neck-of-the-woods back in the 1950s. I guess they are still hovering about, wondering what happened to our neighborhoods over the years. Oh, well, to cite the closing lyric from "Dinner with Drac": "Good night, whatever you are."

CHAPTER 5

What It Was, Was Football

"And Friends, I seen that evenin' the awfulest fight that I ever seen in all my life! They would run at one another and kick one another and grind their feet in one another and I don't know what all, and as fast as one of 'em would get hurt, they'd tote him off and run another one on!"—Andy Griffith, "What It Was, Was Football" (1953)

TO SOMEONE from another country, or to a bumpkin like Griffith, or to a little kid seeing the game played for the first time, this description of football is not far off. It all started for me before I was 3 years old, thanks to my dad and his friends, an open field across the street, and to hundreds of Woodmont Grammar School boys who played the game.

One of those young boys, named Bill Wade, was later drafted by the Los Angeles Rams in 1952; in 1963 he led the Chicago Bears to the NFL Championship. Another was Don McIlhenny, who lived just down the street. He became All-Nashville, All-State and All-Southern at Hillsboro High School in 1952, was Sophmore of the Year at SMU, and played for the Green Bay Packers, among other pro teams. He was on Vince Lombardi's

Bill Wade was a Woodmont team kid who ended up playing professionally.

Don McIlhenny (left) was another Woodmont team kid who ended up playing for a professional team. At right is the 1948 Bowman card for Mac Peebles, one of the men who played tackle with the author at his home when he was a kid. Peebles played for the Washington Redskins.

and Tom Landry's (Dallas) first teams. He also played for Curly Lambeau, for whom the Packer field is named. Bob Webb, another neighborhood kid, said you could always see him coming, because he was pigeon-toed. That was a sign of an athlete back then. We all tried to walk that way.

After World War II, the suburbs became a destination for thousands of families, moving there primarily for the neighborhood schools. My folks were part of that group. They had two girls in the 1930s, and by the time I came along in late 1946, our area had boomed as homes began filling with kids. Woodmont had plenty of teachers but only a few volunteered to help with sport activities, or even knew what they were doing. My father, sensing a need for a structured athletic program, began coaching football.

By fall of 1949, his assemblage of kids at Woodmont began a run of two years without a loss. Our local paper labeled them a "Grammar School Powerhouse."

He made sure every child who wanted to play was made part of the team—no cuts, no matter how pitiful a kid was. Some of those kids became leaders in our community. Some went on to play in high school and beyond.

Some eventually quit football, and another, a great athlete named Steve Thompson, died as a result of a head injury sustained while playing for the Hillsboro Burros in 1955. It had to weigh heavily on my dad.

I became somewhat of a mascot for that group and watched them play and scrimmage at the school, as well as across the street on Herbert's Field. Robert Webb recalls one such scrimmage was against the cheerleaders. Evidently school officials allowed this, with the stipulation that each team limit the physicality of play. Webb said there was an inordinate number of penalties for "piling on" and for "illegal use of the hands."

I spent many an autumn afternoon helping my father get that field ready for play. I "walked the line" many times. This is a process whereby a string is attached to a stick at one end and is stretched some 100 yards and stuck into

The original caption from a 1949 Nashville Banner: "GRAMMAR SCHOOL POWER HOUSE—This array of Woodmont grammar school football performers ended their season Thanksgiving Day with a neat 42-0 win over the MBA Microbes and thus remained unbeaten in Nashville grammar school play. Three of the victories came last week when the BGA seventh and eighth grade team fell 12-6, Franklin's grammar school bowed 19-0, and then Stokes was taken 41-7. Besides the wins above, Woodmont has beaten Parmer twice, Burton and Peabody. Their only losses were to BGA and Franklin, the same two clubs they polished off last week. From left: Front row—Bill Thackston, Lou Powers, Milton Komisar, David Herbert, Robert Webb, Stanley Frank and Carlin Rolfe. Standing–Coach Tommy Henderson, Jerry Cornelius, Max Pollack, Bobby Lineberger, and Jack Herbert."

The 1949 Woodmont team is pictured on Herbert's Field. Back row (left to right): Frankie Drowota, Reber Bolt, Alan Meadows, Mack Rolfe, Jerry Cornelius, Max Pollack, Bobby Lineberger, Wayne Walpool, Carlin Rolfe, Tom Cook, Steve Thompson, Bill Finnell, John Peterson, and Coach Tom Henderson (the author's father). Middle row: Jack Butler, Jackie Lovell, Jack Herbert, Bob Scales, Tim Treanor, Bobby Shaver, Charlie Trimble, Steve Wood, Jerry Cooley, Flem Smith, Norman Minick, Jim Kellum, Marshall Polk and Dick Scales. Front row: Richard Cummings, Bill Thackston, Judson Batts, Lou Powers, Al Strayhorn, Milton Komisar (with the author, Tommy Henderson III, in his lap), David Herbert, Robert Webb, Bill Ingram, Paul Davie and John Ryman. Absent: Tommy Frist. (Images: Tom Henderson)

the ground at the other end. I would often walk that line, mashing it into the ground so that a grown-up could bring out that metal contraption and spread white, powdery lime over the string to mark the boundary. That, and watching practice, became a regular activity for me.

After each workout those kids, like clockwork, crossed over Westmont Avenue, which ran beside our home. They would slowly angle from Herbert's Field through our gravel driveway, around to the back of our house where we had a hose pipe attached to a spicket. It was the source of instant relief, as no water was allowed during practice. To this day I can still hear the sound of cleats and see those kids, sweat streaming down their faces, in grass-stained shoulder pads and khaki practice pants, holding scratched and marred helmets in hand, standing in line waiting to get a drink. Witnessing such a regular spectacle gave me a quiet sense of security over several decades. I felt that as long as there were kids practicing football in Herbert's Field and venturing into my backyard for a cool drink, all was right with the world.

You could say football formally began for me in our living room where, on many occasions, a game took place. I instigated these, but my father went along. He made sure all the furniture was pushed back to avoid the catastrophic, head-into-the-corner-of-the-table injury. He would be on his knees as I took off by the fireplace, at full speed, and tried to cross the imaginary goal line that stretched from the Magnavox radio, across the rug to the last leg of the piano. This was great, as my sisters were self-exiled to their rooms when this event occurred. My dog Red, sensing violence, begged to be put outside. Dad often chose right before suppertime for this activity, so that my mother would be in the kitchen and not standing in the doorway with hands on her hips in disgust. He was no dummy.

When weather permitted, it was outside for a game with friends in our backyard or at the Haury's lot that adjoined our yard through a hedge row. Often Dad would have an acquaintance or two over, and they would play tackle with me. I really never knew any background on some of them other than that they were fun, huge, and loved to roll in the grass. Charley Hoover was one of those gentlemen. Years later, I discovered he co-captained the Vanderbilt team and was drafted by the Detroit Lions as a center/linebacker in 1947. Mac Peebles was another one. He went to Columbia Military Academy, then to Vandy, where he played end and signed up for the Army after the Pearl Harbor attack. Injured in combat, he was nonetheless drafted by the Washington Redskins and played from 1946 to 1951, all with shrapnel in his hip. He also played for Bear Bryant, among others. He was a big guy, just like Hoover, standing 6 feet 3 inches. To me he was 7 feet. These men were gentle giants.

I didn't really know much about my dad's exploits, either, until the high-school years, because he never said anything about them. These men, those older kids from Woodmont, and Herbert's Field, were part of my early pigskin influences.

I was the quarterback on our makeshift team of Woodmont kids during my third- and fourth-grade seasons while my dad attempted to instruct us in the proper techniques of each position. We practiced, with no real schedule looming, in the same field, where just a few years earlier our idolized predecessors roamed.

Lining up with me were Sam, Ed, Paul, Mighty Mouse (John Tompkins), Woodsie, Alex, Willie, Andy and Shap. When I entered BGA, for the seventh and eighth grades, things became increasingly more intense. We were at the bottom of the food chain, designated "sub-freshman."

There were new kids, new coaches, and new fields to practice on. The old cardboard shoulder pads and Styrofoam inserts you put into your pants seemed to be more substantial. Drills, such as "Bull in the Ring" and "2 on 1," were daily rituals.

One drill dictated the coach kick the ball to one of us, some 40 yards away, with instructions to run over the defender who was waiting to engage. Whom you were to tackle was of the utmost concern. Bert Brown, the most feared runner in our class, received the ball on a dead run, while non-athletic Jimmy Ellis was next up as the would-be tackler. It was a disaster in the making. Bert, with a full head of steam, plowed into young James just as both ducked their heads. With a bang, a double knock-out occurred. Our coach, John Bennett, ambled slowly out to help those kids up. Concussions aside, both fell back into line and waited their turn for another go. I do not remember Jimmy playing into his high-school years.

As the freshman quarterback in practice one afternoon, I had the misfortune of handing the ball off to my halfback, Bert, on a sweep play. As I stuck the ball into his midsection, his helmet bar entered my helmet on the right side of my face, breaking both my nose and my cheek bone. One-bar helmets were the norm. It was so subtle he never knew it happened until everyone saw me squirming in pain on the field. It was not a good date night after that.

Later that same year, in a regular game, I went into punt formation, received the ball, took three steps forward and attempted to kick the pigskin away, when one of my blockers, young Calvin, moved too far back, resulting in my foot kicking him in the buttocks and causing the ball to fall harmlessly to the turf. A broken toe, sore anus, and a first-and-ten for the opponent were the end results. Not a highlight of my career, nor of Calvin's, for that matter.

The older I became, the more attrition played a part. I did manage to continue into my sophomore year playing, on the highly-prestigious B-team, coached by "Goat" Smithson. As the signal caller of our squad on a trip to CMA in Columbia, I accomplished a rare feat—a pass to myself. I took the snap and moved to my left and threw a bullet that careened off a stunned, opposing lineman's head. The ricochet sent the oval back to my arms as I

At left, the author (right) plays football with neighborhood friend Josh Ambrose. At right, the author "walks the line" at Herbert's Field, part of the process of marking off the field of play. Powdered lime would be put down on the line.

sprinted for a substantial gain. It was one of my few completions.

That same season, my most glorious feat on the gridiron resulted in mayhem one cold afternoon. It was a five-touchdown production against hapless Central High on their field of rocks by the State Fairgrounds. As the deficit mounted, frustration set in. Subsequently, I was blindsided out of bounds by a disgruntled Golden Tornado, causing a two-team pile up. I remember nothing more about it except that we won convincingly—the game, that is.

Beginning the 1963-1964 season, as the first varsity practice concluded, I was met under the goal post on J.B. Akin Field by our varsity basketball coach, Jimmy French. A decision was put forth: "Either you play football or you play basketball." As I was just 5 feet 10 inches and 145 pounds, and had received numerous injuries, there was not much to decide.

And so ended my illustrious run of football. No running through hoops, or entering the field to the sounds of pep bands, or basking in the adulation of hundreds of fans and adoring cheerleaders. That was it. From then on, it was Pile Drive (slow-motion football), pick-up games, and basketball.

I, like many kids at the time, was now just someone who played the game, a statistic. We lifted very few weights, and for the most part took no muscle-enhancing concoctions or steroids. You brought your size and attitude to the field, whether big or small, and you were coached and played to your abilities.

Back then, it was football at its purest. We played for the love of the game. I am just one of millions of kids who was fortunate enough to have had the opportunity to suit up during those few special years.

CHAPTER 6

Home Cooking

"Hey, Grandpa, what's for supper?"
"Here's what's on the menu tonight:
"A big pot of goulash, filled to the brim,
"And a batch of spoon-bread, to please any whim,
"Turnips from the garden, cooked in cured pork meat,
"Homemade chocolate pie, my what a treat."
—Grandpa Jones, "Hee Haw" (1974)

MY DAD called meals and soups that were a mixture of a bunch of stuff "goulash," but me? I never really knew what it was. Ground beef, noodles, tomatoes, onions, garlic cloves, black pepper, salt, tomato sauce, cheese, green beans, paprika, and whatever else, was all cooked, combined together, put in a dish, and served along with Mom's hot-water cornbread. It was a meal in a bowl.

As a little kid, I am not sure if I liked it or not, but I can tell you that when it was all cooking, the smell made your mouth water. A lot of it probably had to do with something called Crisco, a vegetable shortening introduced in 1911 as an alternative to lard (animal fats and butter), which she regularly spooned into a cast-iron skillet. To this day, that smell takes me back to a good time and place of my youth in the 1950s, a time where my feet barely touched the floor at the supper table.

Eating as a family was a big deal growing up, and so was eating what you grew, or raised. My grandparents in Franklin had a huge garden full of leafy goodies and plants, especially tomatoes. We would pluck them off the vine, rinse each one with spring water from a hose pipe, salt them down and bite.

Pictured in 1917, the author's father feeds the chickens at his family's farm on Lewisburg Pike in Franklin, Tenn. The chicken house is on the left.

Juice went everywhere. It was goo-oood.

Going all the way back to when my dad was a little tot, they had chickens, and lots of them. I recall gathering fresh eggs from the chicken house. The hens that no longer produced usually met their demise by having their necks wrung and being fried-up in a heavy pan with a big glob of lard, just as nice as you please. In their kitchen, just inside a screened-in porch and pantry, Mimi had this wood-burning stove where all the meals were fixed. I ate many a holiday and Sunday meal out there, afterward lusting for the homemade boiled custard. Unfortunately, mine had no bourbon in it. I took care of that during my teens.

Meals were often prepared by Charity, a long-time cook and maid and second mom to Dad and his sister. During my sister's time, the job was filled by a "birthing mother," who lived right across Lewisburg Pike, named Hattie Bridges. Hattie was a wonderful cook. She also had a parrot that all the kids wanted to go see, which was allowed only under strict supervision, because Mr. Parrot was a pecker. All body parts were fair game to that fowl.

Hattie's corn pudding was something else: two eggs, two large ears of corn, one tablespoon of sugar, one-quarter cup of milk and one large lump of butter (whatever a "lump" meant). She separated the eggs, beat the yolks, added some salt and then the rest. Cook at 300 degrees for about an hour, and voilá—scrumptious corn pudding.

As the seasons moved from summer to fall, our kitchen in Nashville seemed to take on a different persona. In the summertime, with the windows all open, most everyone living close by got a good whiff of what you were going to eat. We didn't have a Vent-a-Hood (an over-the-stove air-filtration device) until the late 1950s, so all the aroma, good and bad, permeated the neighborhood and our house. By the time colder weather rolled in, all of our windows and doors were shut. For some reason, this time sticks out more in my memory.

During those late afternoons, while playing outside until dark, I would get the familiar whip-poor-will whistle by my mother, alerting me that it was time to come to supper. Should I not respond immediately, which was usually

The author, holding what is probably a cup of homemade boiled custard, enjoys a holiday meal with his grandfather in 1956.

The "mess of greens" often seen soaking in his mother's sink reminded the author of the science-fiction horror movie "The Day of the Triffids" (1962).

the case, my dad would give the ear-shattering, four-fingers-in-the-mouth whistle. Animals ran for cover when that happened. The Herbert kids, on the next street over, had a large outdoor bell that their folks would ring, audible over a two-block area. "I didn't hear you call" was not an excuse. After finally heeding the alarm and getting hungry, I usually made my way through a couple of backyards and up our side steps right into the kitchen, where the double sink, under the window and right by the door, was always full of water with a mess of greens floating about. Fresh turnip greens, which Mother had meticulously examined one by one, seemed to be a part of the sink. It was as if when our sink was installed, it came with a bunch of mixed greens.

In 1962, after watching the science-fiction gem "The Day of the Triffids," in which large, carnivorous plants attacked regular folks, I briefly dreamed that our floating greens rose from the sink and wreaked havoc in our neighborhood. I awoke just in time to avoid being devoured.

The water and salt the greens soaked in, plus whatever was simmering and cooking on the stove, made for foggy, moisture-laden windows in several rooms. Dr. Carl Seyfert, the 1950s weatherman on WSM-TV Channel 4, should he have been alerted to the situation, would have issued a travel advisory.

Supper was served at a specific time, and everyone was expected to be all washed up, seated for the evening meal, and ready to give thanks for what we had. My dad was a no-nonsense blessing guy. I liked that. His went: "Bless this food to the nourishment of our bodies, and us to thy service, amen." Mothers did the cooking, everyone did the eating, and at our house we were expected, when old enough, to help out with the washing and drying of the dishes. That is another story in itself (see "Washing Dishes" in the book "Yesterdays").

We also had to eat what we were given, and sometimes what we were given was not at the top of my list. For instance, from my mother's recipe book, given to her when she got married in 1934 by my great Aunt Irene Wilson, comes this family favorite, simply labeled: "Luscious Liver (and I really mean it.)" The ingredients: eight slices calves' liver, not too thin; salt and freshly-ground pepper; flour for coating the liver; one onion, sliced; three tablespoons minced green pepper; half a stick of butter; milk; bacon slices; one tablespoon flour; half a cup of consommé; half tablespoon Kitchen Bouquet; one tablespoon worcestershire sauce; one tablespoon minced parsley; and one or two tablespoons sherry, optional (for most adults the sherry was no option; a quart of sherry would not have been enough in my book).

That "luscious liver" graced our supper table every so often and was a real gagger of a meal. When it was time to say the blessing in this case, I secretly asked the Lord to "forgive me for all my bad habits and not to make what I was about to eat upset my stomach, amen." It is no wonder my granddad and dad always had a salt bowl or shaker at their end of the table. I have kept the tradition intact. The salt that is, not the liver. The good thing about having liver for supper is that all meals after that had to be better.

Preparing the meals sometimes required all hands on deck. There was a lot of hand-and-knife work in our kitchen, no Veg-O-Matic back then. There was coring out fresh tomatoes, slicing squash, and chopping garden onions.

It was all fairly simple handwork for fresh turnip greens, which was one thing, but when it came to the stringing of beans, it was quite another. We often called them snap-beans for the sound they made when broken in half. It was not unusual for me and my sisters to have to sit at the breakfast room table, in the middle of which was a large pail of raw green beans, with orders to bust them in half and remove the long string. It was time-consuming but gave me an appreciation of what mother had to do to fix our evening meal. I quickly determined this was not my bailiwick and often thought it was a form of punishment for misbehavior.

Our neighbor, Molly Slabosky, was a real professional at stringing beans. As her son, Alex, recalls: "I remember my mother stringing beans, a practice mostly forgotten today, because the string has been bred out of green beans. This is how my mother did it: 1) Grasp the end of a bean firmly between your thumb and index finger; 2) Twist the tip down toward its seam with a quick, even motion. A fresh bean should snap readily; 3) Draw the broken tip down along the seam to remove the tough fiber that may be present; 4) Snap off the other end of the bean in the same way; 5) Discard the snapped-off ends and any fibers in the small bowl. Place the trimmed bean in the large bowl."

I have to admit, my process was not always according to the numbers, because some long pieces of fiber remained with the bean. It was pretty obvious at dinner, when someone would roll up their lips, place their thumb and forefinger in their mouth and extract a barely visible string. I got the evil eye from Mom on more than one occasion.

When Sunday lunch rolled around, we regularly had roast beef, but on occasion lamb was the main course. My favorite part of having lamb was the mint jelly, as I was not a big mutton admirer. It might have had something to do with the Mother Goose influence of Mary and her little lamb, I am not sure.

We always had a meat, vegetable, dairy and fruit. You know, back then, a growing family needed fats, lard, iron (that tasty liver was high in iron), and Vitamin A and D from milk and cheese. Everyone had to have iron. Television stars in the 1950s and '60s, like Lawrence Welk, Bud Collyer and Ted Mack, told us so. They also said that if we felt run down and tired, to take something called Geritol for "iron poor blood." I suppose it was a way to get iron if you passed on the liver. I don't guess they liked it, either.

Meals had to look good, too. According to the "Betty Crocker's Picture Cook Book" (1950): "It's important to plan a variety of foods for well balanced meals to keep your family well nourished. But above all, be sure those meals are appetizing, attractive, and delicious to eat. For mealtime should help build a happy home life."

I had a happy home life. Looking back, I bet it was because of Betty Crocker. Alex said his mom wore that book out.

With regard to meat, we got ours from the butcher at the A&P, Cooper and Martin, or H.G. Hills.

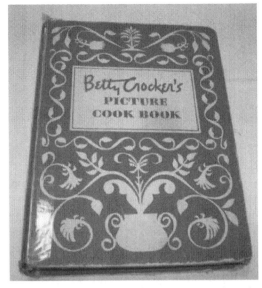

This first edition "Betty Crocker's Picture Cook Book" (1950) was used by neighbor Alex Slabosky's mom.

Freezers on refrigerators were not very big back then, and if you did not have a stand-alone freezer, you had to either grill or eat it right away, or do as Alex's folks did. They rented out a freezer locker in Green Hills, about where the Bluebird Café is now.

"My father would buy beef from the butcher, have it cut and wrapped and then stored in the freezer locker," Alex said. "We would go to the locker and take home packages of beef that we planned to use in the next week."

I will say this: His mother's roast-beef gravy was the best ever. Who knows what was in it, but when it was cooking and I happened to be in their house, I could smell the aroma and would always make a bee-line to the kitchen, where she would graciously give me a tablespoon to taste. It was probably nothing more than simmering beef juice and salt, but it was one of those childhood things you don't forget, kind of like the pickle-juice popsicles I once made. Those were not a huge favorite, and made most of the neighborhood kids' lips pucker. Not many forgot those, either.

On weekends, weather permitting, my father would fire up the charcoal grill in our patio and throw on a huge piece of meat, announcing to the neighborhood, via smoke signals like we saw in those western movies, that

This Rival meat plate was used by the author's father to hold charbroiled meat. The grooves led to a collection spot at the bottom, which was good for "sopping up gravy and juice."

there was some good eating fixing to take place. I remember that big bone in the middle was the best part. When our entrée had cooked enough to his liking, he would place it on a Rival Mfg. Company 11-inch, footed, cast-aluminum, meat-sizzle-serving plate, to be specific, one that sported little channels into which all that juice collected. Whenever Mom got that platter out, I knew there was going to be tasty, grilled meat for dinner. After most of the prime stuff had been carved away, and all eaters had their fill, I would pick up that bone and gnaw away at what was left. The meat that was the best tasting, my Pop told me, was the part next to the bone. Forget the fact that there was fat around it. He said he always ate that part growing up, and he lived to be over 90. I ate it, too, much to the disappointment of our dogs, who sat close by with unbelievable patience.

You combine this charbroiled meat with tossed greens, hand-cut potato salad, fresh sliced tomatoes, those hand-snapped string beans, Mom's homemade potato rolls, a big pitcher of sweet, southern ice tea (steeped with lemon and mint), and top it all off with peach cobbler and homemade, hand-cranked ice cream, and you were good for a few days. You just had to be sure there was some Sal Hepatica in the medicine cabinet.

WEEKDAYS, ON school nights back in the 1950s and 1960s, supper included about everything. Mothers back in those days could do more with less than most any time in history. At our house, when it wasn't something fresh-bought, it was leftovers we ate. Actually, "Leftovers" were a menu item at our place. That habit of saving all that went uneaten came from conserving everything during the war years. A good example was homemade vegetable soup. Several hours of boiling some kind of bone was the first step in making it, after which who knows what went into the pot. The shiny film floating over the simmering broth was grease from the bone and was not removed. Lord help our arteries. However, it made for some tasty stuff. I am not sure how they lived so long back then, but my mother made it to 96, Dad to 90. Maybe our current health "experts" need to revisit those times.

On particularly busy days, when there was not enough time to spend hours in the kitchen, Chef Boy-Ar-Dee helped out. He was a real Italian chef whose product line of cheap Italian meals you could fix in a jiffy made him famous. His actual name was Ettore "Hector" Boiardi. He changed his name so American housewives could pronounce it. A smart move. Get this: He supervised the catering of Woodrow Wilson's second marriage in 1915 at the Greenbrier in West Virginia. A 1953 TV commercial featured the Chef touting his spaghetti "entrée" by removing each mouth-watering item from a brightly-colored box; there were noodles, a can of sauce, and a small can of grated cheese…umm, umm. It could be some of the worst spaghetti ever, but hey, it tasted good to me, and kids ate it. A neighborhood pal recalls eating many "Chef" meals complimented with Birds Eye frozen vegetables, canned corn niblets (what in the world is a niblet anyway? I relate it to part of the Jolly Green Giant's anatomy, but I could be wrong), a Betty Crocker homemade cake and some Velvet or Sealtest ice cream. I am almost certain that the Chef's canned Beefaroni was

Chef Boy-Ar-Dee was the brand name of food products marketed by an Italian chef named Ettore "Hector" Boiardi.

The gelatinous "slime" surrounding Spam reminded the author of the science-fiction horror movie "The Blob" (1958). *(Central Archive of Movie Posters)*

not served at the Greenbrier. I couldn't find any news accounts of a restroom stampede during the event.

I am not sure why, but lurking about in our pantry was always a can of Spam—or its wannabe, Treet. It was deemed a meat product, loosely, I might add. When you sliced a piece of Spam (if you could ever open it with that key you had to use to peel back the top) and put it on white bread with lettuce, tomatoes and mustard, and combined it with a can of Vietti chili, you had yourself a real gasser of a meal. This was not gourmet dining. By the way, I am not quite clear on what makes up Spam, but "pork by-products" doesn't sound good. And I'm pretty sure that the slime surrounding the rectangular pork loaf doesn't fit into one of the major food groups. I always thought it resembled the creature from "The Blob," which was a 1958 science-fiction gem starring Steve McQueen, about a large gelatinous mass slowly chasing teenagers. The trailer stated: "It Eats You Alive." I made sure that stuff was cleansed away from my Spam. I had no intention of being eaten alive by a Jello-like substance.

My school lunch experience was quite memorable, especially during the elementary years. Incidentally, the recipe notebook given to my mother in 1934 when she first got married included a miscellaneous section with pre-typed suggestions, one of which was entitled "Cold Lunches For School Children." Two scrumptious selections were recommended for mothers with young kids. Remember now, this is 1934. Here is the first: "One cottage cheese sandwich on brown bread; 1 jelly sandwich on white bread; 1 orange; half-pint bottle of milk." The second nutritious suggestion was: "One egg sandwich on whole wheat bread; 1 raisin sandwich on white bread; celery; 1 cup custard." Man, oh, man, what I wouldn't give to go back in time and have those lunches to take to school. I can tell you one thing, no one would swipe those from your lunch box.

> *There's a food goin' around that's a sticky sticky goo*
> *(Peanut, peanut butter)*
> *Oh, well, it tastes real good, but it's so hard to chew*
> *(Peanut, peanut butter)*
> *All my friends tell me that they dig it the most*
> *(Peanut, peanut butter) ...*
> —The Marathons, "Peanut Butter" (1961)

What was mainly packed in my lunch box was either the standard, go-to peanut-butter-and-jelly sandwich, which was liked by most all kids, or a tuna-fish sandwich, complimented by some type of fruit, a raw stick of celery or carrot, maybe an apple and something else sweet. The canned tuna most popular back in the 1950s was Chicken of the Sea. The can featured a blonde mermaid with a scepter for visual effects. It attracted all the males. Television ads featured Charlie the Tuna, representing Star-Kist Tuna, who made his debut in 1961. I am not sure which one I ate, because they tasted the same to me, but I did like Charlie, because he was an animated cartoon fish featured in brief ad skits on television. Chicken of the Sea was less expensive, so that is probably what I got. "Sorry, Charlie," as the ad would say.

Back then our sandwiches, whether tuna, bologna, pimento cheese or peanut butter and jelly, were mainly wrapped in wax paper, because aluminum

This advertisement for Chicken of the Sea tuna appeared in a 1952 "Family Circle" magazine.

foil was pricey. There were no baggies, Ziploc bags, and stuff like that. As far as a drink goes, I did have a thermos inside my Hopalong Cassidy lunch box, which was often filled with milk and never Kool-Aid. That was really not a good choice for an already high-energy child.

Taking a lunch to school that your mom had fixed was one thing, but chowing down in the school cafeteria was quite another. At my school, Woodmont, Mrs. McClure with her ever-present hair net was in charge. All meals were prepared right there, on site. There wasn't any far-away commercial location where food was cooked and delivered. No, sir, everything was fresh and prepared in our school's kitchen under her supervision. An hour or two before it was time for lunch, those familiar smells would make their way throughout the halls and drift into our classrooms. You could almost predict what was on the menu.

In an orderly fashion, each class would enter the serving area, and one by one we would grab a hard plastic tray from a tall stack, place it on the long metal bars (that stretched seemingly forever) and begin our trek down the line, eyeing all the good eating, under the watchful eyes of several ladies all dressed in white aprons. I forget how much it cost to go through the line, but it was not much. A few coins would get you a meal. A lot of kids had those rubber, squeeze-open, palm-sized coin holders that looked like a mouth opening up, while others used whatever method was convenient. Edward Mendelsohn was the subject of much ridicule for bringing his money in a long tube sock. I am not even sure it was a clean one, either.

"Lunch ladies" observe a typical lunch line in a school cafeteria of the 1950s.

Our silverware was the authentic stuff, nothing plastic. We also had real glasses and plates, believe it or not. The plates were real china, but I am certain it was the lowest grade possible, because kids had a habit of dropping stuff.

Jello was served as a staple at Woodmont, at all grade schools, and at our homes. There was an endless supply everywhere. It was the ubiquitous treat. Red Jello with sliced bananas; green Jello with canned pears; yellow Jello with canned pineapple—the combinations were endless. As for me, I used that little wooden spoon to scoop out the vanilla ice cream from those pull-tab cardboard cups we got at school, and dump it on top of my favorite, red Jello, for an a-la-mode-type effect. You could slurp it down, too, making it especially easy on the gums, particularly if you just had those metal braces put on. There was not much chewing required.

Always on the menu were those small cartons of Jersey Farms, Purity and Anthony sweet and chocolate milk. Those peel-back cartons gradually phased out the glass bottles of the prior decades. Occasionally there were orange and grape drinks in similar small cartons, often nestled in a bed of shaved ice. A large bin of spaghetti and meat sauce got the best attendance award. Chef Boy-Ar-Dee it was not. This was freshly-made, Davidson-County

Italian cuisine. Of course, some kids had to say there were worms moving about, which caused gullible children to keep moving on down the line. Pal Alex said there was always peanut butter, chili, bar-b-que, Ritz crackers and pickles. He told me he and his classmates would make pickle-cracker sandwiches that they "would cram into our mouths." Just the visual of that leads me to believe that some table manners were compromised.

As you moved your tray down the line, on display were real mashed potatoes, homemade pasta and freshly-made cookies. Artificial ingredients were unheard of and not served, because health experts believed they caused behavioral problems and decreased learning capacity. When I got a "U" (unsatisfactory) for Deportment on my report card, I blamed it on the Sugar Pops cereal I ate. That excuse did not work, by the way.

There were hamburgers, meat loaf (probably remnants of ground beef left over from the burgers), macaroni, hash casseroles, fried chicken, homemade soups, always a bin of oranges, apples and bananas and various ice-cream cups and frozen delights. There was also a dessert that made a frequent appearance— tapioca pudding, a creamy conglomerate of unknown ingredients that, I am told, did taste pretty good, although to me a spoonful of the delicacy resembled something you might see on the school playground. I passed on the tapioca.

The Woodmont School cafeteria/auditorium is pictured here during a 1965 graduation banquet. After use, the dining tables would be folded up and stored in the wall indentations seen in the upper right.

Eskimo Pies (chocolate-covered vanilla ice cream bars on a stick) were big hits. Alex remembers this little event concerning whom I believe to be Mrs. Clark, a cute teacher especially fancied by all us boys:

"Our fourth-grade class was housed in an old, temporary (not portable) classroom located behind the teachers' parking area behind the school building. Our teacher was young and inexperienced, and we convinced her to let us collect Eskimo Pie wrappers and save them in a spare desk in our classroom. Every day after lunch we would collect the wrappers and put them in the desk. After a school break, Christmas, or spring, I don't remember which, we came back to find bits and pieces of Eskimo Pie wrappers on the floor, and when we pulled our collection of wrappers out of the desk, they had been gnawed into shreds by mice who had been attracted by the chocolate remains on the wrappers. Our wrapper collection project ended then and there."

I guess Mighty Mouse and his pals were forced to dine elsewhere.

I'll tell you what else was always offered, and that was the ever-present salmon croquette, rectangular, too. It was a fish staple and appeared like clockwork on Fridays. I often wondered in which pond you could catch a rectangular salmon, because I had never seen one that shape. I eventually passed over that thought and just forgot about it.

After making our selections, and paying at the front, we would make our way into the auditorium, which doubled as our cafeteria, and take a seat with our class and our teacher at the green tables and benches that, when not in use, folded up into the walls. Wise adults figured that if our teacher sat with us it would prevent poor table manners. Smart move. It worked for the most part; however, if you really wanted to toss a lima bean at someone, or eat pickle-cracker sandwiches, conniving kids found a way.

What I never forgot was being too close to classmate Bob Creighton, in the second grade in 1954, when he threw up his entire lunch after biting down on a Band-Aid that had been cooked inside of one of those salmon croquette patties. Witnessing bar-b-que, succotash, and the remnants of the half eaten fish up-chucked all over the long green table, partially spraying Barry Levine and Mary Rogers Chambers, put an abrupt end to my appetite. A lightning fast evacuation to drop off our trays and uneaten lunches at the return window ensued as Bob's teacher, Miss Elsie, ushered him off to the infirmary. While he was being led away, and in an attempt to make him feel better, I told him that he would be all right, because the Band-Aid had been fully cooked. It didn't work. He rolled his eyes at me and threw up again. I don't think he wanted to hear that.

What a great childhood memory.

Don't sit under the apple tree,
with anyone else but me,
Anyone else but me,
anyone else but me,
NO NO NO!

—Glenn Miller Orchestra with Tex Beneke, The Modernaires and Marion Hutton, "Don't Sit Under the Apple Tree" (1942)

OUR NEIGHBORS had two apple trees in their back yard that regularly produced fruit. Sitting under them would get you a bop on the noggin. Those apples that were not yanked off and used as projectiles by urchins on the block formed the basis for homemade apple crisp, apple pie and apple sauce. My

Bay Henderson, the author's mother, poses by the family plum tree with a bounty of plums. They were used by her to make juice and jelly for Christmas.

mother made apple pie, too, highlighted by long, thick strips of sugar-coated pastry crisscrossed on top of the apples and filling. I topped mine off with some vanilla ice cream, which, in my eyes, made my slice extra scrumptious.

> *Little Jack Horner*
> *Sat in the corner,*
> *Eating a Christmas pie;*
> *He put in his thumb,*
> *And pulled out a plum,*
> *And said, "What a good boy am I!"*
> —Mother Goose (circa 1660)

I never knew Jack nor had much in common with him, except that I did have to sit in a corner from time to time, although it wasn't for sucking my thumb or for pulling a plum out of my mouth. It was probably for throwing them. It is best we forget about that. At our home, we did have this productive plum tree that sat right next to our driveway. My mother would pull off the plums, pick up the ones that had fallen, and do her thing in the kitchen to make plum jelly, juice and whatever else for her friends and neighbors for the holidays. The tree itself bloomed almost every year and was sometimes pictured with family members standing beside it. Fortunately, there are no family photos showing me sitting in a corner…that I can find.

The following statement, about Southern cooking back in the day, is pretty much dead-on: "Here in this smiling valley of the Harpeth River in the heart of Tennessee, the people of Williamson County and the town of Franklin like to think that the sun shines a little brighter, the moon's rays are a little softer, birds sing a little sweeter, flowers are a little prettier and the cooking is just a little better. Here, Southern traditions are cherished. Woman is still the heart of the home and the kitchen is the heart of the house."

This was on the first page the recipe book given to my mother by my grandmother. "The Harpeth Valley Cook Book" of 1953 contained "tried and true" recipes compiled by the St. Paul's Episcopal Woman's Auxiliary in Franklin, Tenn., where my grandparents lived. While thumbing through

Page 25 of the "Harpeth Valley Cook Book" (1953) was well used by the Henderson family.

it, I came across a page that was extremely stained and worn. Page 25 was a treasure trove, featuring two delicious pies that our family regularly consumed. The chess pie was my favorite but so was the long-forgotten Confederate pie. Those two non-dietetic delicacies were so good it would make your forehead sweat. Running laps around my grandmother's chicken house or taking off on my bike, when at home, was a post-pie-eating requirement. Let us just say that there was no scrimping on sugar, eggs and butter.

What I did scrimp on was pigs' feet, and other unidentifiable animal parts floating in a jar of formaldehyde-like fluid, that often stared at me when I opened my grandmother's refrigerator. I knew my granddaddy would occasionally take a nip or two of whiskey, and now I know why. I came across this recipe in the same book, and have an idea what some of those body parts were used for: Hog's Head Cheese. The description said it was a creole version of souse. Souse, mind you, is meat from a cow's face or heel, chicken feet or pig's face, shoulder, feet or knuckle. Lord help us. In case you have a hankering for this tasty treat, here is the recipe and instructions: "Boil hog's face with 4 hog's feet in water seasoned with salt, red pepper, bay leaves, allspice. When meat is tender, remove from water, grind or cut very fine. Put meat in pot with lots of chopped green onions, parsley, more salt and red pepper and add enough stock to make very moist. When thoroughly heated, pour into molds to congeal."

Congeal? This isn't Jell-O. Perhaps this serving suggestion could have been added: It is highly advised that all guests should drink heavily before consuming. Good gracious.

When Thanksgiving and Christmas came around, seasonal items began appearing. One I will never forget was cranberry ice. Mother served it in tall parfait glasses with ice-tea spoons. It was kind of like frozen ice cream. In her recipe book of 1934, I found out how to make it. Many of her old recipes were copied by my sister Lynn in 1956 as a form of therapy to help her recover from a near-fatal car accident. This was one of them: "$1 1/2$ quarts of cranberries in water, $1 1/2$ lemons, $1 1/2$ cups of sugar, 2 whites of egg. Cook cranberries until all to pieces. Strain, add sugar while hot. Cool and add to lemon juice. Add more sugar water and lemon if desired. Add whites of egg, well beaten. Freeze."

It was good stuff. You could readily tell there was no holding back on sugar. "Well-beaten" required getting out the mixer, which eventually meant I got to lick the beaters. That was always the best part, particularly if it was cake or cookies in the making. For kids, licking the beaters were at the top of the eating cycle.

Also appearing during the holidays were a couple of items that fell into my nauseating category. Both were a favorite of my father. One of them was what I have learned to be a vegetable plant of some kind called rhubarb. My dad ate rhubarb pie, which, though sweet, was ghastly and ranked high on my gag-o-meter. I avoided it like it was poisonous, which in fact it was, or at least the leaves were. The stalks were used to make this "dish." It was one item I was not forced to eat, because upchucking at the supper table was frowned upon.

Here was another holiday staple that showed up on our dinner table: spiced round, a specialty meat originating here in Nashville in the 19th century. It basically was beef stuffed with pork fat, brined, and spiced with a special mixture of cinnamon, allspice, cloves and brown sugar. Butchers larded the beef with pork fat (using special needles to inject spiced lard into the meat) and then boiled and simmered it. Any roast, steak, or meat of any kind that has been seasoned and injected with lard, sugar, cinnamon and the like was, and is, an item that my digestive system reacts to in a negative fashion. Count me out. I think our spiced round came from H.G. Hills and was made

In this 1935 photo of an H.G Hills grocery store, a container of spiced round (a local favorite at Christmas time) can be seen along with pickled pigs feet, kraut and picnic hams. (Don Henry)

by Jacobs Packing Company. The only redeeming quality spiced round had, in my opinion, was the appearance; it was roundish, kind of like a whole ham, and had small white squares all over it and in it. It was a holiday regular on our table, but not in my stomach.

During those festive gatherings, a whole turkey was always placed in front of my dad for him to carve. In later years, my brother-in-law and I gave him a little relief, for just an occasional holiday or two.

Dad was the chief carver. I always sat to his left. My guess is that this particular seating arrangement was set by my mother, so that if in the rare circumstance I happened to display poor table manners, he could easily stick me with a fork. I learned good table manners. Everyone waited while he sliced the white and the dark meat, as plates moved around in circular fashion from one family member to another. One sister sat to my left, followed by mother at the head of the table closest to the kitchen, and my other sister, who sat to her left on the other side of the table. Guests and future family filled in. I usually started the plates moving after my dad put the turkey on each one.

This was a big responsibility. As a youngster, I took this task with the utmost care. Heck, without me, I thought, no one would eat. I was a big shot.

Another favorite of his and mine, that sat in a casserole dish in front of me, was escalloped oysters. This dish was comprised of raw oysters that had been oven baked with layers of salt, crumbled saltines, butter, and oyster liquid. It was fine eating to us "men"; however, most of the ladies determined the sliminess was most unappealing. Their loss. My dad and I made sure there were no leftovers.

> *Gimme (gravy)*
> *On my mash potatoes*
> *Gimme (gravy)*
> *C'mon an' treat me right*
> *Gimme (gravy)*
> *Baby, you're the greatest*
> *So gimme, gimme, gimme, gimme, gravy tonight.*
> —Dee Dee Sharp, "Gravy (for my Mashed Potatoes)" (1962)

There were also no leftovers of mashed potatoes and homemade stuffing, which could include anything from bread crumbs and cornflakes to celery. They went down extra fast when drenched with a couple of ladles of mother's special gravy. No one really saw what went into the gravy except my sisters, usually. One time I did slip into the kitchen to see her making it, and because it was so good, I determined not to let what I saw influence my eating or damage anyone else's anticipation of the upcoming meal. It was always called giblet gravy. The definition of giblet by Webster simply states: "An edible, visceral organ of a fowl, usually in plural." Had it been announced at the table that the gravy consisted primarily of a multitude of internal organs of the deceased bird we were about to eat, there might have been a boycott. It was simply referred to as giblet, a term we had heard but were unclear as to the meaning. We accepted the term as being a part of the holiday season.

To make this giblet stuff, Mother placed a small pan on the back eye of our Hotpoint stove and added a brownish liquid, which was brought up to bubbling status. That liquid consisted of water and drippings from our turkey roasting in the oven. Into that, she added possibly the following organs and such: the gobbler's long neck, I think the heart, a liver and the gizzard. The gizzard is defined as a modified muscular pouch, behind the stomach in the digestive tract of birds, having a thick lining and often containing ingested grit that aids in the breakdown of seeds before digestion. Unbeknownst to us, we were about to ingest grit, too. Oh, well—no one knew it and it tasted great. No harm, no fowl.

No part of our 20-pound bird went to waste. I was told children in China were starving to death; therefore, every consumable part of our meal had to be utilized to its fullest and all us kids had to clean our plates. I often wondered if Mom bagged up what we didn't eat and mailed the scraps to Chairman Mao. Just as the giblets were harvested for the gravy, the bones, cartilage and other unchewables were utilized in other dishes. My favorite was turkey soup, made just a few days after the main event. Most all of the bones, back, wings, upper joints, gristle, cartilage, and meat too tough to eat, along with chopped garlic and pieces of onion, carrots, and celery that were baked in the oven with the turkey, were all put in a huge caldron, sprinkled with ample amounts of salt and pepper, and boiled for hours. The resulting broth was then strained into another large pan, where rice, green beans, tomatoes and the excess meat that had gone uneaten were cooked again until mother saw fit to serve it. The shelf life was unlimited. By the way, even the residue that was strained was not thrown out the back door of our kitchen and over the porch (a procedure reserved for the dirty dishwater). Those cooked remnants were mixed in with Ken-L Ration and gobbled up by Red, Chris, or other canine on duty at the time. Hey, Thanksgiving, Christmas and the holidays were for everybody.

"Everybody," to my mother, was a loose term and was not exclusively family. Also included were those whose loved ones had recently passed on. My mother was always taking leftovers and freshly-made goodies to some poor widow, or family member, whether it was during the holidays or any other time. It is as if she went through the obituaries, picked out someone she didn't know within a relatively short driving distance, and took over some sort of meal or casserole. I can just visualize her knocking on the door of such a person and saying, "Mrs. Honeycutt, I am Bay Henderson. You don't know me, but I noticed your husband just passed away. I am so sorry for your loss.

In this December 1970 photo, the author (right) carves a turkey with his brother-in-law, Arville Wheeler. The chore was usually reserved for the author's father.

Here is a big pan of my Swedish meatballs." That was Mother. For some reason, we Southerners seem to console folks with food.

A note to all: Should I happen to enter the land of endless turkey soup and beaters covered in icing, please have mercy on my surviving kin folk, close friends, and saddened relatives by forgoing your desire to make them feel better with certain foods. The last thing they want to hear, particularly around the holidays, is: "Hello, my name is Bobby Joe Crabtree. I didn't know Tom personally but just thought, to help ease y'all's pain, I would bring you folks over some fresh-made hog's head cheese and rhubarb pie." For God's sakes, they sure don't need a stomach ache during the grieving period.

CHAPTER 7

The Gators

I WAS A lot like many kids. During the waning years of the 1950s, I often, clandestinely, tuned in to the late-night sounds coming out of WLAC-AM radio. It was different. It was "black" music— a blues-infused sound not heard before on mainstream radio; a sound that spread across the South like ripples in a country pond. Artists that we white boys had never heard of now became names we knew, while the soulful guitar and deep-rooted vocals touched a part of us that had never been touched before.

Disc jockeys John R., Gene Nobles, and Hoss Allen—with their "black dialect" in sayings like "Lord have mercy" and "I got to do it"—pioneered these "new" artists to a growing fan base all across Dixie. Names like Elmore James, Solomon Burke, Earl Gaines, Howlin' Wolf, T. Bone Walker, Jimmy Reed, Ligtnin' Slim, Sonny Boy Williamson and Arthur Gunter were just a few.

"I used to listen to WLAC 1510 growing up. I loved the blues. That probably had as much influence on me as anything as far as playing the guitar," said Ed Hoge, founder of The Gators combo.

It was not only the blues, but those harmonic doo-wop songs Hoge listened to that had a lasting impact on his music career: Five Satins' "In the Still of the Night," The Dells' "Oh What A Night," The Penguins' "Earth Angel," El Dorados' "At My Front Door," The Cadillacs' "Speedo," The Del-Vikings' "Come Go With Me," The Skyliners' "Since I Don't Have You," Mystics' "Hushabye," Silhouettes' "Get A Job," and The Rays' "Silhouettes."

"I loved doo-wop," Hoge said.

Adding more influence were the performances of a band called the Casual Teens, whose leader, Buzz Cason, was an Isaac Litton kid who got

In this 1959 publicity photo for The Gators are (left to right): Ed Hoge, Wayne Stagg, Pete Townes, Jerry Tuttle and Billy Edwards. (Ed Hoge)

his start lip-synching on Noel Ball's Saturday Showcase shown on WSIX Channel 8 television. The later named Casuals were showmen and became known as Nashville's first rock-and-roll band. Mac Gayden and the Sliders, with Chuck Neese, were performing all over town, too, and were a bonafide top-tier combo as well. It now was time for Hoge to start his own band.

It was 1958, at age 16, when he gathered together two Hillsboro High School classmates, Wayne Stagg and Pete Townes, and drummer Billy Edwards, to form his own combo—one he labeled The Gators. "The Gator" was actually a risqué dance started in the mid-1950s that involved a writhing, hunching motion. It and "The Dog" had the dubious distinction of being the only dances that were prohibited on American Bandstand.

Hoge said: "The Gators was my idea, and, in all honesty, there was no rhyme or reason to it. I just thought it would be a cool name and everyone went along with it."

I am not sure I buy that explanation.

The Gators' first gig was at Belmont Methodist Church, at a sock hop in the gym. Ed strummed his Fender Musicmaster guitar to doo-wop, rhythm and blues, Chuck Berry, and songs of the day before a crowd of young teenagers. Their payday was close to $50, plus a lot of applause. It was a huge ego trip. Shortly thereafter the group added a saxophone player, Kossie Gardner, and later Oscar "Jack" Jackson. Jerry Tuttle, who came from Malden, Mo., joined in after those guys, and the boys were off and running.

When asked if the main reason he started the band was girls, Hoge responded: "It was the love of the music, but…anybody that says they didn't love the adulation is lying."

That first performance got them some recognition, and, like other combos across the city (see "Combo Crazy" in the book "When I Was a Kid"), they began to play fraternities, sororities, high schools and local colleges.

Pat Patrick, who had just started his own band, The Saturns, recalls, "I heard them many times sneaking into backyards and at the Bellevue Roller Rink [The Chicken Coop]. I was impressed by Ed's vocals, Tuttle's sax solos,

The Gators in 1962 (left to right): Dewey Martin, Wayne Stagg, Pete Townes, Ed Hoge and Jerry Tuttle. *(Ed Hoge)*

and Pete's humongous Rickenbacher bass. They were fantastic."

In 1959, Hoge's father, recognizing his son's keen interest in music, particularly the blues, treated him and his date to an evening at Hettie Ray's Dinner Club high atop Nine Mile Hill. It was not just an outing with Dad, but a night to remember, because that night blues great Arthur Gunter—Hawaiian shirt, alcohol and all—performed his famous "Baby, Let's Play House," along with his complete repertoire, to an overflowing crowd.

"It was a big deal. I loved Arthur Gunter" Hoge said.

When I asked Ed who his date was, he replied immediately, "I don't remember who she was. I guess she didn't make much of an impression."

Arthur stole the show.

As The Gators' reputation grew, so did the gigs. Their shows began to stretch throughout the state and into others, as well.

"We played all over the South, into Alabama, Mississippi, and farther west," Hoge said.

A Hillsboro High chapter of the SPO fraternity scheduled them to play at a combo party that their Arkansas chapter attended. Steve Hall, a member, said they were so impressed that they called him when they got back home, wanting to hire them for one of their parties in Forest City. Hall put them in touch with Pete Townes, and they were booked for a big dance in Arkansas.

Hall said: "Made me feel good, because The Gators were not only a really good band, but they were really nice guys."

In the early 1960s, the band regularly made the 200-mile trip to Memphis down Highway 100, entertaining for proms at the Peabody Hotel in the Continental Ballroom. When asked how the accommodations were at the hotel and how they and their instruments moved from place to place, Hoge responded: "I have no idea [about the accommodations]. We packed up and drove back after the show. Our equipment was transported in a U-Haul-type trailer that was all green with 'THE GATORS' painted in white lettering on the side."

Up until 1962, the kids cruised to their shows in Hoge's 1957 Chevy that he bought in 1959, but by 1962, thanks to their newfound fame, he was able to by a brand-new hardtop Chevy Impala Super Sport. Nice.

Hoge did all the scheduling for the band in his monthly, "At-A-Glance" notebook, even though he was now living in Murfreesboro and a student at MTSC (Middle Tennessee State College).

When asked which school he booked that had the wildest parties, Hoge said, without hesitation, the University of the South (Sewanee). In 1961, he set up a show for the Phi Gamma Delta fraternity for a Friday night and a Saturday night.

"They put us up in the Gailor Hall dormitory," Hoge recalled. "It was one of the wildest weekends we had."

No detailed explanation was given…just as well.

Locally, there were several bands that were arguably considered the most popular in the very early 1960s. Three of them were The Sliders, The Gators, and the Monarchs, all of which occasionally competed with each other in what was called The Battle of the Bands. Excluded from that group was Charlie McCoy and the Escorts because, as Ed put it, "They were in a class by themselves, nobody could touch them."

The Gators were no slackers themselves. In 1961, Hoge's disc jockey idol, Noel Ball, came calling with a record deal. Ball was a producer along with his hosting duties on television and radio. He inked them to a contract with Dot Records, which was said to have been the first signing ever of a rock-and-roll band by that label. Their instrumental "Sunburst" was subsequently released and enjoyed a Top-40 listing, although it didn't come without apprehension, for as Hoge said, "I'm surprised we did not get sued, because it sounded so much like 'Rebel Rouser' and Duane Eddy."

He was not kidding about that. The B-side of that high-energy tune was "Canadian Moonlight."

It was also in 1961 when The Gators' landscape changed. Give credit to New York group Joey Dee and the Starliters and their record entitled "The Peppermint Twist." It elevated the Peppermint Lounge, at 128 West Ave. and 45th Street in Manhattan, to legendary status. Part of the song went like this:

> Well meet me baby down at 45th Street.
> Where the Peppermint Twisters meet.
> And you'll learn to do this, the Peppermint Twist.
> Bop shoo-op, a Bop, Bop, shoo-op

Original caption from a June 1962 Nashville Tennessean: "GONE GATORS: Home grown rock 'n' rollers returned to the Black Poodle for the fourth engagement this week, where they're booked for eight solid weeks. The Gaters say road trips are fine, but it's great to find success in your own home town. The group is composed of Wayne Stagg, Steve Bess, Ed Hoge and Jerry Tuttle. Their latest hit was 'Sunburst.'" (Ed Hoge)

The song went to No. 1 on the charts and Peppermint Lounges sprang up all over the country. In Nashville, the Black Poodle in Printer's Alley became known as one.

During this time, Hoge was playing in the band, going to class, and arranging gigs on the weekends from Murfreesboro when "somehow we got contacted by the manager of the Black Poodle, John Carney—known by all as a shady individual—and he hired us."

Hoge recalls going to meet him at the Poodle.

"We walked past the smoke-filled dance floor and dimly-lit interior, up some stairs that ascended to a door, where Carney not only had his office, but his living quarters as well."

If you were concerned about fresh air, this was not the place. Carney signed The Gators to be the house band six nights a week for an extended

The Gators are featured on signs for The Black Poodle Peppermint Lounge in Printer's Alley in 1963. (Ed Hoge)

stay, with the stipulation they were to be paid in cash only. That was good by the boys, and probably good for Carney and the Black Poodle.

This was a game-changer. Hoge knew he could not commute nightly back and forth between the two cities, so he transferred to Peabody College, taking classes only in the afternoons.

"I took six quarter hours, because we were playing until 2 a.m., Monday through Thursday nights, and until 3 a.m. on Fridays and Saturdays," Hoge said. "Obviously, I couldn't go to school in the mornings."

This time period, of 1962–1963 at the Black Poodle, saw The Gators with a few different band members. It was still Ed Hoge, Pete Townes, Wayne Stagg, and Jerry Tuttle, but Dewey Martin had replaced Billy Edwards. Martin only stayed a few months, leaving to join Buffalo Springfield. Not a bad move. Steve Bess eventually took Martin's spot and fit right in. The boys didn't miss a beat.

Back then, liquor-by-the-drink was illegal, so clubs were supposed to offer "set-ups" while the patrons brought their own bottle, but, not surprisingly, rules were breached. The Black Poodle was no exception, imagine that. In the summer of 1962, the police conducted a massive raid inside the club, arresting 16 customers and confiscating over 700 bottles of liquor.

"They came in when we were playing," Hoge said. "We were not cuffed, but the place was closed down, temporarily of course."

Hoge and thee colleagues were banned from playing there, because they were minors. Never underestimate the power of knowing the right folks, for they got what was called a "Removal of Minority," approved largely "because one of our member's father was a good friend of Wilson West, an attorney who was the brother of then Mayor Ben West," Hoge said. "Our defense claim was that we should not be deprived of our livelihood, and we were not partaking of any alcohol."

All parties agreed, including the parents, and the motion was granted, allowing the kids to retake the stage and keep pumping out their great sound.

A quartet called the Four Seasons released the blockbuster song "Sherry" in August 1962, followed by another monstrous hit, "Big Girls Don't Cry," in October, and in January 1963, they released another chart-topper, "Walk Like A Man." These songs added additional firepower to an already dynamic Gator combo, primarily because Hoge had a God-given falsetto that was dead-on like that of Frankie Valli, the lead singer of Four Seasons.

Needless to say, a Four Seasons set became a regular part of the show. Hoge will never forget that the Four Seasons were playing at the Municipal Auditorium one night, and, after finishing their sold out performance, Valli and Bob Gaudio, having heard that a local band was covering their songs, showed up at the Black Poodle to catch their routine. Word is they were floored.

"I don't mind saying," Hoge said. "I'm bragging, but we were damn good on the Four Seasons. We nailed the Four Seasons."

When The Gators show ended in the wee hours, the band had to go somewhere to eat breakfast, usually to the Noel Café, which was open 24 hours and was a popular spot for the late-night crowd. Many times the hostesses and waitresses of the Poodle ate there as well.

Hoge observed: "The waitresses looked really sharp, sitting around the bar in the darkened Black Poodle, but in the daylight of the Noel, well…they didn't look near as good."

The band, however, always looked sharp, buying their clothes from world famous Lansky Brothers in Memphis, the same place Elvis got his. When asked what type of shoes they wore, Hoge said nothing sporty, but admitted they once did have a pair of those Flagg Brothers with the lightning bolts on the sides. I hate to admit it, but so did I. I was styling.

As the Peppermint craze died down, and the band's extended engagement expired, the boys moved on. In 1964, they played at Fort Knox and for clubs at Fort Campbell, Ky., such as the Top 5 Club, The NCO Club, and the hottest and most raucous club on the base, Club Jinmachi, which was just for enlisted men of rank E-4 and below. I was one of those E-4s-and-below in later years and can testify that when a dynamite band or act like The Gators performed, and the three-percent beer was slugged down by the gallons, socially-deprived soldiers could get a bit rowdy. Hoge acknowledged as such.

During this period, Hoge finally concluded it was time to pursue his dream and leave the band, so he gathered his belongings and moved to Memphis to enter the Southern College of Optometry. Steve Bess took over the group, and The Gators became Steve Bess and The Gators, and later just Steve Bess, dropping The Gators name for good in the 1970s.

Ed joined up with Tommy Burke and the Counts from 1965 to 1967, while in Memphis, and played alongside Thomas Boggs (later of the Box Tops) and keyboard player Bobby Whitlock (before he joined Derek and the Dominos). Hoge played his

This ad for The Gators' regular gig at the Black Poodle in Printer's Alley appeared in the June 1, 1962, Nashville Banner. (Tennessee State Library and Archives)

last note with Burke's Counts in 1967 and left the band scene permanently upon receiving his doctorate degree. He spoke of his decision to practice optometry rather than continue playing in a combo: "It was a no-brainer, what with all the student loans and time I had invested in it, plus I couldn't do both."

Then he hesitated and confided: "I hated to quit."

Speaking for Hoge and his Gators, the opening lines of a Four Seasons hit seem fitting:

> *Oh, what a night, late December back in '63,*
> *What a very special time for me…*

For all those kids who shing-a-linged on driveways, mash-potatoed in gyms, slow danced in ballrooms, and twisted the night away in clubs and bars, I am certain that period was special for them, too, particularly when a Nashville band called The Gators turned it loose…Lord have mercy!

CHAPTER 8

The Blizzard of '51

PATTI PAGE'S "Tennessee Waltz" would have been a fitting theme song for the winter storm that hit Nashville during the last days of January and the first week of February 1951. Waltzing is about all one could do on our streets, thanks to the worst ice and snow storm to ever visit our city.

The frosty event began Sunday, Jan. 28, with rain pelting down most of the day. The temperature was as high as 59 degrees before a frontal system moved through. Temperatures fell below freezing that night and into Monday, creating a mix of freezing rain and snow. This posed some motoring problems for workers but was manageable, as less than two inches of the mixture accumulated and no more fell on Tuesday.

Wednesday and Thursday were a different story. Five inches of sleet and snow came down on Jan. 31, followed by another five inches of snow on Feb. 1, covering Nashville with a layered, frozen blanket of nearly a foot. "A Bushel and A Peck," sung by Perry Como and Betty Hutton, one of the most listened to recordings of the day, would have been a comical way of referring to the combined accumulations.

The author, at age 4, stands by his frozen basketball net in an image taken from an 8mm home movie.

Power outages ravaged

This February 1951 snapshot of ice-coated trees and snow-covered cars captures the famous blizzard. (Tennessee State Library and Archives, Ralph G. Morrissey Collection)

the city as the temperature dipped to a record-breaking −13 degrees on Feb. 2 followed by −10 degrees the next day. Windy conditions added to the misery, and the city was, for all practical purposes, shut down.

Many coal companies, unable to make deliveries, were relegated to self-serve status. WSM television went off the air. We missed parts of the second season of "The Lone Ranger." "Ozzie and Harriett," "The Stu Erwin Show" and kid favorites Kukla, Fran and Ollie and Howdy Doody all had to be replaced with quality family time, causing much consternation within some households, I am sure.

The original caption from the Feb. 3, 1951, Nashville Banner: "One-Horse Open Sleigh: Also back to fundamentals were Mr. and Mrs. Sam L. Jones of 4707 Granny White Pike, who hitched up horses and sled for a journey to the grocery store. With them are Jimmy and Phil Pitts of the same address." (Nashville Public Library, The Nashville Room, photo by John Malone)

On Feb. 3 the Nashville Banner, on a limited work force, published a single eight-page edition containing no advertising. Reports included collapsed roofs, closed businesses, and a transportation system reduced to emergency vehicles. Airline flights were cancelled for days. Hundreds of telephone and power lines were downed due to sagging branches and falling trees.

Phil Morgan's father was a supervisor for Southern Bell Telephone and Telegraph during that time. As he recalls, "I don't remember seeing him for a couple of weeks."

If there was a "Chattanooga Shoe Shine Boy" (a chart-topper by Red Foley at the time), he was probably without customers as rail service slowly stopped. Foley, who lived in Nashville, recorded one of the top gospel songs in history that year with the Sunshine Boys. Its title perfectly described the scene in outlying areas of town: "(There Will be) Peace in the Valley (For Me)."

Our new neighbor up the street, 31-year-old Bill Baker, pulled on his metal buckled galoshes, donned his vintage cap and ventured out to observe the spectacular scenery. He remembers standing at the intersection of Woodmont Bloulevard and Estes Road marveling at the collapsed, iced trees and the snow-covered streets. It was the middle of the day, but there was no sound or motion as far as he could see. The serenity was something that has not been forgotten. There truly was peace in the valley.

I had just turned 4 years old when the storm crippled the city and was more or less oblivious to everything going on around me. I knew only that it had snowed and it was fun.

Our electricity went off during the first few days of February, rendering our coal furnace useless. A continuous fire maintained by my dad in our living-room fireplace kept us warm, dried out wet socks and hats, and provided a place for Mom to prepare hot meals.

My father, complete with his leather jacket and Dick Tracy hat, pulled me around on a sled in our front yard amidst fallen tree limbs and calf-high snow with our dog Red sitting in my lap. My sister Lynn was the accomplice who "encouraged" Red to enjoy the ride. My low basketball goal in the back yard had its net frozen stiff. Each strand of nylon was a glistening piece of ice that when pulled moved all the other strands in unison.

The original caption from the Feb. 1, 1951, Nashville Banner: "Come and Get It: Many Nashville coal yards have been largely on a self-service basis during the big freeze, with customers doing their own picking and shoveling. Left to right are Mrs. Ray Coats and her husband of 4111 Saunders Ave. and James Ivey of 312 Twenty-first Ave., North." (Nashville Public Library, Nashville Room, photo by Warren Gallenbeck)

My other sister, Beth, met up with neighbors Teddy Fore and Lucy Van Ness. Judy Siegriest, whose family made the finest pies in town (Siegriest Pies), also joined the kids, along with the Cooleys. The complete gang, with their trusty American Flyer sleds in tow, trekked approximately two miles to join other out-of-school kids on Westview Avenue to brave the steep grades and curves of that street. The folks living at the top of that hill lit a huge bonfire (the smoke could be seen for blocks) and provided hot chocolate to keep the icy teenagers warm and in good spirits.

The house at 610 Wilson Avenue was the new home of Bill and Ruth Baker. Their 5-year-old daughter, Emily, was in the front yard with her father building a snowman on the third day of the blizzard, when an unusual noise and then an equally odd-looking vehicle came up their snowy street. As no automobiles could navigate the roads, the strange machine immediately attracted their attention. As it came closer and finally stopped in front of their home, Bill recognized it as a Studebaker Weasel, the kind used in WWII to traverse rough terrain. A National Guardsman in full garb emerged. With the icy precipitation raining down, he asked directions to Cantrell Avenue, which was just one

The original caption from the Feb. 3, 1951, Nashville Banner: "Need Any Ice Today? Ice was all in the day's work for (left to right) Bill Haskins, Buford Overton and Edward Ivy, making routine deliveries on frozen routes for the American Service Co. They reported little difficulty in keeping their stock from melting." (Nashville Public Library, Nashville Room, photo by Warren Gallenbeck)

This snapshot is dated February 1951 and was possibly taken near the photographer's home on 25th Avenue South. (Tennessee State Library and Archives, Ralph G. Morrissey Collection)

block away. Bill asked what was going on. The soldier said a report had come in that a family was without power or food and needed rescuing. Even though I lived on Cantrell at the time, I have yet to find out which family it was. Bill likewise never found out. He gave them directions and watched as the olive drab, front-wheeled vehicle with a tank track on the rear moved on down Westmont Avenue, flinging high quantities of snow as it disappeared.

The Bakers were also without power and transportation and short on staples themselves. Bill's attempt at scrambling eggs over soft coal that he burned in his fireplace turned out looking great, but had a taste like Nashville's "Smoky Joe" skyline smelled. Those scrambled goodies were quickly discarded, much to his wife Ruth's delight.

That event, coupled with a dwindling food supply, resulted in a bit of resourcefulness. Bill's childhood Flexible Flyer sled was the eye of his ambition. He attached a long board to the rear, grabbed the rope on the front, and proceeded down the snowy road to the neighborhood Cooper and Martin grocery store on Harding Road, some three-quarters of a mile away.

Just after purchasing the much-needed provisions and loading them onto his sled, a man, who appeared to be in his 60s, approached Bill. He asked if,

Ice pulled telephone lines to the ground during the Blizzard of '51. (Tennessee State Library and Archives)

for a price, he could share his sled to transport food items to his home. Bill acquiesced on the condition that the gentleman help him pull the sled back up the hill to his home. The man agreed. They both grabbed the rope and began clogging back up Woodlawn Avenue. But Bill soon realized that most of the effort was his, as his new "friend" turned out to be less than energetic. A quick solution was devised—Bill slowed his pace and pretended to strain while pulling the sled. Taking the hint, the neighbor started pulling his share, and the heavily-loaded makeshift grocery cart finally made it back up to the Baker's home. Gathering up his items from the sled, the now perspiring and weary neighbor thanked Bill and continued his snowy journey on foot to parts unknown.

Phillip Wright was an 8-year-old lad living with his parents and three brothers at the Military Classification Center on Sidco Drive off of Thompson Lane in 1951. Though it was freezing cold inside their poorly-insulated apartment, the sub-zero temperatures outside created some opportunities for the kids.

The soft coal piled up in a central location on the grounds had frozen solid, making shoveling an aerobic exercise. Phillip and his brothers used picks to dislodge the pellets, which were to be used in their wood-burning stove. While outside, they noticed that ice had accumulated on the neighbors' wooden steps. This danger became a source of income quickly realized by the kids. Using their picks, hatchets and shovels, they cleared each residence's steps, often taking as long as an hour. Phillip said they relied on the generosity of the renters for compensation. A nickel was pocketed on average, but occasionally fifteen cents was distributed. Those particular neighbors were thought of as "well-to-do," and were mentally noted for other chores that might arise.

Sleds, snow skis, and even a one-horse open sleigh were used to navigate around our city during this event. Nashville's most famous jeweler back then, Harold L. Shyer, also a noted gin rummy expert, resorted to an unusual measure just to make sure he did not miss his weekly card game with friend Herman Johnson. Shyer lived at 229 Lauderdale, and Johnson lived down the hill at 3903 Valley Road. Transportation being non-existent and the street unsafe to set foot upon, Shyer enlisted a couple of youths to push him on their sled down the hill to Johnson's residence. The word from Harold was that he survived the journey. I guess, "If Harold Says It's So, It's So!" to revive his famous advertising slogan. No word on how he made it back up the hill.

Over on Golf Club Lane, almost everyone was cold and in the dark, that is, except the Cassety family. Mr. Fred Cassety, I surmise, remembered the second biggest snowfall of 15 inches just 22 years earlier in 1929, and he had buried all of his power lines underground. In 1951 electrical lines going from the street to each individual home were the norm. During the storm, ice-laden tree branches felled these small lines, resulting in loss of power. Cassety, owner of Cassety Coal Company, had his home coal furnace in high gear and his electric

Devil's Elbow or Paradise Ridge in Joelton is shown covered in ice during the blizzard. (W.C. Midgett)

heat cranked up. Fires were going in the main part of the house, making for a wonderful gathering spot for neighboring families. His 12-year-old son, Fred, said everyone had a great time. Kids came in and out of the snow from sledding to get hot chocolate and warm up, while adults came by to visit and partake of hot vittles. Homeowners got to know one another, while, prior to the blizzard, they may not have even met. People slept in several rooms of the house, turning the Cassetty home into a make-shift boarding house, free of charge, no less, thanks to the generosity of the family.

After a horrific traffic jam caused by citizens trying to get downtown for overdue shopping and work, life eventually retuned to normal. Newspapers came back full force, and subscribers could once again enjoy comic strips like "Little Orphan Annie," "Gasoline Alley" and "Li'l Abner." Families who had televisions on Feb. 8 were able to watch the first local telecast of "Your Hit Parade," featuring Snooky Lanson, which aired on WSM Channel 4.

Sleds were put away, snowmen disappeared into soggy yards, and autos with chains still on their tires started making that familiar, loud, clanging, jingling noise on iceless streets. Schools reopened, parents rejoiced, and weekly card games resumed. The last of the ice and snow melted by Feb. 12, and the Blizzard of '51 became one for the ages.

CHAPTER 9

Hitchin' a Ride

A thumb goes up, a car goes by
It's nearly 1 am and here I am
Hitchin' a ride; Hitchin' a ride
Gotta get me home by the morning light,
Ride, ride, ride, hitchin' a ride
—Vanity Fair, "Hitchin' A Ride" (1969)

I EXPERIENCED THOSE words, four years earlier in 1965, on a desolate strip of highway in rural Florida. A friend and I, just kids at the time, were at the mercy of whomever would give us a lift some 70 miles down the road to our destination. No need for details, but it involved some spirits, a U-joint falling out of my MG, and a desire to get to a football game. I had several hitchhiking episodes during my misspent youth, most of them coming from necessity.

In this 1931 photo, three boys try to hitch a ride. (Corbis)

In a famous scene from "It Happened One Night" (1934), Claudette Colbert uses her feminine assets to attract a ride while Clark Gable looks on. (Wikipedia)

To fully appreciate hitchhiking, one needs to know that asking for a ride by sticking out your thumb was more or less an American phenomenon. Our invention of automobiles in the 20th century began to supplement trains, horses, and wagons of the 19th century and became the preferred mode of transportation for those who had the wherewithall to afford them. Citizens with no vehicle would simply stick out their thumb and "ask" for a ride. A New York Times story in 1927 stated that hitchhiking "appeals strongly to the imaginative young American who wants to see his country as he crosses it and must do so cheaply."

When the Great Depression hit in the late 1920s, hitchhiking accelerated. It was not uncommon to see entire families thumbing for a ride. There was even a Transit Bureau set up to help hobos and hitchhikers. A scene in the 1934 movie "It Happened One Night," starring Clark Gable and Claudette Colbert, accentuated hitchhiking during that time period. As vehicles kept passing the stranded couple by, Colbert became frustrated and decided to hike up her skirt. A motorist immediately screeched to a halt. Hitchhiking, somewhat because of that scene, became an accepted method of transportation.

In 1937, the Sunday comic strip "The Squirrel Cage" featured a character called the Little Hitchhiker, who was derived from that film.

During my 1965 hitchhiking event, my rolled-up pants did little to stop traffic...thank goodness for that.

When the Depression ended and WWII started, it became patriotic to give a serviceman a ride heading towards his old country home or trying to get to town on a three-day pass. Etiquette queen Emily Post once mentioned that it was patriotic to give female defense workers a lift to work during the gas-rationing days.

In the very early 1950s, hitchhiking waned a bit. But my generation, labeled restless and adventuresome, reinvigorated the practice. Most strangers we rode with were friendly, and the folks that we picked up often were just going home or to work, usually in the same town or in the adjoining community. For teens it became kind of romantic and sort of James-Dean rebellious to hit the two-lane with your thumb out, particularly out west if you were "hitching" with a surfboard. Unfortunately for me, the surf scene on Richland Creek was scant and my thumbing adventures were not even remotely romantic, plus I for sure was no James Dean.

Living some 20 miles from school in 1960 and having just begun the eighth grade, my main transportation was catching our school's bus at a designated spot. A daily 40-minute ride through the country to the small town of Franklin, Tenn., was all part of the package. Five or six of us kids would gather early each morning at Lynnbrook Road and Woodmont Boulevard and impatiently wait for the bus to come over the hill. Having spare time, especially when the bus was behind schedule, was usually not a good thing for a bunch of 12-year-olds. One morning we determined that it would be really neat to grab a handful of loose, BB-sized pebbles that were strewn about, and loft them high in the air far in advance of oncoming traffic. The gravel was just small enough to be undetected by the eye, but loud enough to be heard by us kids. If hurled properly, our projectiles would make windshield contact several yards down the road, removing us from suspicion, we thought. This exercise became part of our routine, until one morning when our rocks, which had grown in size, careened off a 1950-ish Ford. The fellows in the car immediately slowed, stopped, and U-turned. Imagine that. As the gentlemen spewed words never heard on "The Adventures of Ozzie and Harriet," the five

The Gilco Drive-In as pictured in an advertisement in the 1960 Franklin High School annual. (Tom Henderson)

of us, with satchels, backpacks, hats and books in-tow, scurried off in all directions. Fortunately, we skedaddled away in time and found hiding places, all except poor Jim, that is, bless his heart. A portly youngster, his limited speed enabled the irate motorists to apprehend him while he was huddled behind a forsythia bush somewhere in the Doyles' backyard. The rest of us, too afraid to return to our stop, hitched a ride with nice folks who believed that we just happened to miss our bus. We acquired several demerits for being late, while Jim's life was spared after receiving a thorough scolding from the two motorists, who personally escorted him to school. After learning about the rock flinging, our headmaster administered an epic whipping to Jimmy's backside. Lord only knows what all he got when arriving home that night.

Demerits became part of my schooling, and I regularly accumulated at least three on a weekly basis. You see, my school gave each student two merits at the beginning of each school week, kind of like a buffer for demerits received that were sometimes questionable. In my case there usually was no question; I earned them. Receiving three demerits meant you had to stay after school to serve off that extra hour, always on a Friday.

One particular Friday, in the fall of 1960, was no exception. Spending that hour in study hall caused me to miss the bus, so, rather than call a parent and thereby acknowledge my misdeeds, I and a friend in the same predicament, Mike Meloan, decided we would hitchhike home to Nashville. We had made it through Franklin to Hillsboro Road, just past Five Points and beyond Gray's Drug Store some 500 feet or so when Mike did something really stupid. Here we were, with our backpacks strapped on, our coats tied by the arms around our waists, sleeves rolled up on our nice tab-on-the-back shirts, trudging along with our thumbs out on a crisp fall afternoon. Traffic was bumper-to-bumper on the opposite side of the highway all coming into Franklin, either from Franklin High School, work in Nashville, or just starting the Friday cruise scene early, when Mike notices a hot rod full of duck-tailed, cigarette-smoking youths creeping along about 15 miles an hour. In all his infinite wisdom he says to me: "Watch this." He then proceeds to yell "Hey!" at those teens and flicks them the middle finger. Not the middle finger by itself, mind you, but the middle finger with two fingers bent on either side. This was worse than an ordinary "bird," because it meant something unspeakable. What that was, I wasn't sure, but I had seen and heard about it from older boys.

Well, it turns out those kids were part of a local rough-neck gang called the Sundrops, who regularly hung out at the Gilco Drive-In just across the railroad tracks from my grandparents' home on Lewisburg Pike. Upon seeing Mike's gesture, the driver jammed his breaks (forgetting that he was in heavy traffic), and a '58 Ford behind blasted them into an older couple in a mid-1950s Chrysler, crumpling their rear end. The Sundrop vehicle had the back windshield knocked out and both front headlights shattered, in addition to the hood getting mashed in, while the car

In "The Hitch-Hiker" (1953), two fishermen pick up a sociopath on the run from the law who tells them he will kill them when they are no longer useful. (www.classicfilmaficionados.com)

that hit them had dark plumes of smoke coming from the engine. It was a multi-car pileup.

Amidst this chaotic scene of broken glass, smoking engines and pieces of auto parts strewn about, I turned to Mike and said something like "Holy sh--, we got to get outta here." Both of us sprinted as best we could, despite all of our school paraphernalia bouncing on our backsides, for the nearest business. It just happened to be the Thompson-Morton Rambler auto dealership owned by a classmate's father. Into the showroom we ran, gasping for breath, and told the management what had happened and that the feared Sundrops would be coming after us. Someone then told us to hide in the back of the building. Sure enough, within minutes, part of the gang came in asking if anyone had seen "two kids with backpacks come running this way." After the coast was clear, we were driven out past the city limits and beyond in one of those old Nash Ramblers, as we lay under a blanket in the back seat.

Now out of town, we could feel a slight sense of relief; unfortunately, it was to be short lived. As we once again began to thumb for a ride to Nashville, a fellow in a '54 Ford pulled over, offered us a lift, and we hopped in the back seat. He told us his name was Benny Pewitt and that he worked at Pewitt Brothers Gulf on the Columbia Pike. That was all well and good, except Benny was in the midst of happy hour, as evidenced by the pungent smell of bourbon in the ice-filled glass that rested on his dashboard. As he sipped while passing folks on hills of the two-lane road to Nashville, his ability to maintain the speed limit and stay on the proper side of the pike became increasingly compromised. By the grace of God, somehow Benny managed to make it into Davidson County to the rise just past Harding Place overlooking Green Hills. Emerging from the floor board of the back seat, I said: "You can let us off here now, and thanks for the ride." He pulled over, said good-bye, and drove away. Somewhere close to the Green Hills Market we found a phone booth and called our parents. From then on, when I missed the afternoon bus, I did not hesitate to call home. As a matter of fact, I always had a ride lined up or told my folks in advance.

Those Sundrops never spotted us on the highway again and, as I recollect, I never frequented the famous Gilco again, either.

The feeling I would die in an accident with a high-flying gas station

A man hitchhikes at the city limits of Waco, Texas, in November 1939. (Library of Congress, photo by Russell Lee)

attendant made me think of a chilling episode of the television program "Alfred Hitchcock Presents," in 1960, entitled "Hitch-Hiker," and another one from the show "The Twilight Zone" called "Hitch-Hike," with the famous line "Going my way?" from Death himself in the back seat.

There were a lot of movies and songs that either depicted hitchhiking or had hitchhiking in the title. Some were positive, and some portrayed the dark side of thumbing. "Hitchhike To Happiness" was released in 1945, followed the next year by "The Postman Always Rings Twice." The flick "The Hitch-Hiker" in 1953 gave everyone pause. It featured two fishermen who pick up a hitchhiker, a psychotic, escaped convict who informs the men he intends to kill them when the ride is over. In the 1950s, a book called "On The Road" romanticized the practice, so much so that the hippie generation of the 1960s and '70s got wind of it and found it to be a way of rebelling, using others for your transportation. In 1962, thumbing a ride was so popular that Marvin Gaye recorded "Hitch Hike" and Chubby Checker came out with a dance song called "Popeye (The Hitch Hiker)":

> *Well now, clap your hands,*
> *and thumb your thumbs,*
> *That's how the Popeye dance is done.*
> *Popeye.*

Thumbing was still popular into the late '60s and early '70s, but the glamour began to fade with the advancing interstate systems, societal changes of the 1970s and the counter-culture movement. A good example of that was in the 1969 free-wheeling motorcycle film, "Easy Rider," in which two bikers pick up a hitchhiker and transport him to a local commune. That same year The Doors recorded "Riders on the Storm," portraying the dark side of thumbing. Further eroding the allure of hitchin' a ride were several high-profile murders. In particular was the case of serial killer Edmund Kemper, who dismembered six female hitchhiking students in 1972 and 1973. He became known as the "Co-ed Killer." Newsweek, Seventeen magazine and others published articles on the perils of catching rides with strangers, while Good Housekeeping fueled unwarranted alarm by stating that "female hitchhikers practically invented rape." In 1972, Creedence Clearwater Revival's "Sweet Hitchhiker" sang of giving a lift to a girl, while John Denver's 1976 song "Hitchhiker" tried to make folks empathize with the fading art:

> *I'm an old hitchhiker*
> *I wonder what's waitin' 'round the bend.*
> *I don't know what I might see and*
> *I don't need no guarantee.*
> *Just a ride from here to there*
> *And back again.*

Hitchhiking of the 1940s, 1950s and 1960s, as I knew it, was now just a slowly disappearing memory in the rearview mirror. I can tell you this: Having narrowly avoided torture and subsequent death by local thugs, and surviving several near-head-on collisions on Hillsboro Pike at the hands of a soused motorist, I don't ever wonder about anything "waitin' 'round the bend," because from now on, I guarantee you, I will always have "a ride from here to there, and back again."

CHAPTER 10

Saturday at the Y

WHEN YOU are a fifth- or sixth-grade elementary school student, social functions are just around the corner but not yet in full force. Your extra-curricular activities are somewhat narrow in scope, resulting in a lot of idle hours, especially on the weekends. In February of 1959 I couldn't have cared less about St. Cecilia and their big Winter Wonderland dance featuring the Monarchs, or the open combo at Mrs. Brown's showcasing the Sliders. I never read the society sections of our papers for news about fraternity and sorority events. I vaguely remember high-school students going door-to-door collecting for the March of Dimes, and I was not the least bit interested in the appearance at Peabody College of famous panelist Bennett Cerf of the "What's My Line" TV show.

Music was unavoidable in February 1959, as rock-and-roll was the thing and radio was still the main source of listening entertainment. That year I regularly heard Lloyd Price's "Stagger Lee," The Crests' "16 Candles," Jackie Wilson's "Lonely Teardrops" and Frankie Avalon's "Venus." I also could not help but hear about the plane crash in Clear Lake, Iowa, that killed Buddy Holly, The Big Bopper and Richie Valens. Don McLean later said it was "the day the music died."

My Saturday mornings were usually occupied with the "Mickey Mouse Club," "Heckle and Jeckle," "Fury," "Little Rascals," "Ruff & Ready" and other kid-friendly television selections. I did go to movies, mostly the family-oriented fare or some B-grade flicks at the Fifth Avenue or Knickerbocker. I remember seeing Steve McQueen in "The Blob," the story of a slow-moving pile of goo that somehow outran ordinary civilians.

Despite these sources of entertainment, cold, wintery Saturday afternoons usually spelled trouble for the parents of 11- and 12-year-old boys. Fortunately for me and my neighborhood friends, my father belonged to the YMCA.

The Nashville Young Men's Christian Association was originally organized in 1855, at the corner of Cedar Street and the Public Square. In February 1959, it was located in a building at the corner of Seventh and Union, where it looked much the same as when it was dedicated in 1912. It not only provided housing, meals, and exercise for young men and professionals, but afforded a much needed outlet for kids with boundless energy.

Most of my buddies were into sports, particularly basketball, so my father, seeking to keep our home civil and my mom sane, would load up eight to 10 of us Woodmont Schoolers into his station wagon and transport us all the way downtown for an afternoon of fun and energy-draining activity at the Y. Not only did he assemble my neighborhood friends into a team and coach us on our court at my home on Cantrell, but he also made sure we practiced on the court at the Y, where some of our games were played. I am sure all of the mothers were grateful for his tutelage and his afternoon chaperoning skills. As an added bonus, our fifth- and sixth-grade Woodmont Hawks team, featuring most of the same kids who piled into our station wagon on those cold afternoons, won the City Championship,

Rows of wire lockers were used by members to store their equipment. This circa 1960 photo was caption: "Grab a basket! (Each member has his own.) And get ready for the treat of your life." (YMCA Archives)

The Woodmont Hawks are pictured after winning the 1959 City Basketball Championship for boys aged 11 and 12. Back row (left to right): John Williams, Ed Anderson, Tom Weaver, Norman Carl, Alex Slabosky and John Woods. Front row: John Shapiro, Ricky Chambers, Tommy Henderson, Andy Harris, David Carmichael and John Tompkins. Paul Clements was absent due to illness. (Tom Henderson)

going unbeaten both in the league and in the tournament. I am sure spending hours on the Y court was a factor. (The season-ending tourney happened to be played at that downtown YMCA.)

We usually parked in the National Life parking lot some two blocks away and walked to the old brick building, entering on Union Street. One of the first things I remember seeing inside was a group of old-timers huddled around a card table glaring at a worn-out checkerboard. They were intense and a bit scraggly and rough around the edges. They sat off to the right of the lobby next to an expansive set of stairs that led to nowhere, it seemed. I later learned that most of the housing was up those steps. You could get a meal and a room for $3, as I recall. I felt either the room or the meal had to be discounted. I chose to sample neither.

The dressing rooms were downstairs, and each person picked out a wire, rectangular basket that was stacked upon other baskets, a number of which had

In this photo from a late-1940s brochure for the YMCA titled "It's Wise To Be A Y's Man," men play a volley ball game in the gymnasium, above which can be seen the balcony seating and the above that the track level. (Metro Archives)

old t-shirts, athletic supporters and handball gloves stuck in the holes for drying and odor-removal purposes. The drying worked fine but the odor removal was questionable. A pinching of the nostrils was highly recommended.

The excitement of going up to the gym was contagious. Usually there was a game in progress on one end and on the other a volleyball game or some other unstructured activity taking up part of the court. This was always a source of frustration to us as we were helpless to run them off. After all, we were just guests of my dad.

Eventually a goal would become free, and we would divide up and play some basketball. By then my dad had already left us on our own, put on his workout gear and headed up to the handball courts on the roof. After a few spirited games, most of us boys went our own way and explored various parts of the facility. We usually raced each other around the track. We closely passed irritated members at a blistering pace only to have to slow down to catch our breath and watch those same joggers eventually pass us by. It was the old tortoise-and-hare story.

In a photo titled "Barbells" (also from the "It's Wise To Be A Y's Man" brochure), men work out in the facility's weight room. (Metro Archives)

The handball courts were one of the main attractions. I always had to take my friends up there to see my dad play. Getting there was a death-defying adventure. You had to go up the steps from the gym to the balcony seating area, exit there, go up to the track level, which overlooked both the basketball court and the seats, and finally exit out another door to the fire escape some nine or 10 stories up. All of a sudden you were on the outside of the building and had to climb another couple of sets of steel steps to get to a small door that took you to the handball courts. It was quite an exciting trek for any youngster, especially if snow and ice were prevalent. I never knew how many kids had fallen to their death, so I gripped the cold, steel handrails so hard that my hands were numb by the time I reached the summit. We always went up and came down in pairs. The feeling was that if a fall did occur one of us could go for help. Falling by yourself, we figured, could result in days of abandonment on a lonely rooftop several stories below.

There was a weight room where it was most apparent we were not welcomed and frankly had no business playing in there. The standard was to grab the medicine ball and throw it to your friend. We would inevitably pick up a barbell and act like we knew what we were doing and usually got a "You boys be careful in here."

At various points in the club there were contraptions affixed to the walls featuring ropes with handles on the ends enabling you to pull several small weights at once. There were long, thick ropes hanging from the gym roof; we always climbed them but with very little success.

Somewhere off to the side and in a corner was the supposed automatic midrift reducer. This unit was nothing more than a wide belt that wrapped around your midsection and would vibrate you back and forth at the flip of a switch. We used it to make funny sounds, much to the dismay of those waiting to be reduced. There was even a hydraulic machine you could sit in and simulate rowing a canoe.

Then there was swimming. Before reaching the room with the heated pool, you could hear the echoes of splashing kids. One afternoon, with much anticipation, I went back to my locker, put on my suit and raced to the entrance. Opening the door I noticed a lot of fog and immediately felt the warmth of the water. Just as I jumped in I heard "Hey, son!" After coming up for air, I was informed by this middle-aged, towel-wrapped gentleman that I had to take off my bathing suit to swim. Aghast, I looked around and noticed my friends were coming out of their trunks. A sign on the wall said "No Running, No Yelling, No Suits."

So I did as I was told, and I must say it was a feeling of unusual freedom. I felt water flowing in, out, and around areas I never knew I had. A few body parts had never free-floated before. Paul Clements recollects that naked children who ran around the pool often created a flapping sound as they passed by. Eventually I felt at ease, but the more I thought about it, the more a decision to exit and clothe seemed in order. I was not alone and was soon followed by most of my pals.

Former long-time director Jim Rayhab said that concerns about filter clogging from cotton bathing trunks and sanitary reasons prompted the rule. I was also informed later that we all must be aware of anyone who took a dip with an apparent rash. I imagined that the pool would be promptly evacuated should such a sighting occur.

My dad made sure we all took a shower after the day's workout. Taking clothes off in front of your friends was a little uncomfortable but not necessarily a big deal. However, there was the time when one of us stripped, and we all became acutely aware of a marked, below-the-waist maturity enhanced by an inordinate amount of hair. After a few giggles and snide remarks we hit the showers, scrubbed down, dressed, and applied the complimentary Vitalis and Brylcreem ("A Little Dab Will Do You") hair lotions and the familiar Bay Rum body liquid.

We always experienced all there was to do at the Y on many a Saturday afternoon, thanks to my dad. We played some ping-pong in the basement, peeked in the Siesta Room, watched folks bake under the portable sun lamps, looked briefly in the steam room, and even got a snack. The old YMCA at the corner of Seventh and Union was eventually demolished in 1972, and with it went unforgettable good times by a handful of fifth- and sixth-graders.

"Residents Must Vacate" read the headline of this Nov. 13, 1971, Nashville Banner photo. The old YMCA building stood at the corner of 7th and Union, today the location of the Sheraton Nashville Downtown Hotel. Original caption: "Residents of the downtown YMCA have been told they must vacate their rooms by Dec. 9. An Atlanta development firm is expected to announce within several days that a 24-story Regency Hyatt House Hotel, costing in excess of $14 million, will be constructed on the YMCA building site." (Nashville Public Library, The Nashville Room, photo by Owen Cartwright)

CHAPTER 11

Fireworks

BLOWING UP the evening meal will not get you high marks in cooking circles, although that is what one legend says about the invention of fireworks. A Chinese chef, back some 2,000 years ago, was preparing dinner when he mixed charcoal, sulphur and saltpeter and put it into a bamboo container, which he heated over an open flame. The result was an explosion, probably showering the guests with inordinate amounts of noodles and freshly-caught fish. No word on the chef's fate. Years after this cooking debacle, the Chinese began stuffing bamboo and paper tubes with the same recipe to create loud bangs, which was thought to help scare off evil spirits and ghosts. I don't know about the ghosts and spirits, but dogs on my street headed for the hills when we set off fireworks, and, I might add, we were not working on a dinner menu.

It is said that Captain John Adams set off the first firework display in America in 1608 at Jamestown. Over a 100 years later, colonists got a bit loose with those fireworks, according to a newspaper in Rhode Island

Above is the author's very own brick of Black Cat firecrackers, saved from when he was a kid.

in 1731. It said that a ban was to be implemented because pranks got out of hand due to a "mischievous use of pyrotechnics." Kids will be kids, I guess.

On July 3, 1776, the day before the adoption of the Declaration of Independence, John Adams wrote to his wife about the day ahead. In part it read: "I am apt to believe that it will be celebrated by succeeding generations as the great anniversary festival. It ought to be solemnized with pomp and parade...bonfires and illuminations...from one end of this continent to the other, from this time forward, forevermore."

A circa 1900 postcard shows children celebrating the Fourth of July with fireworks. (Corbis)

That July Fourth and every year since, fireworks have become an integral part of that day. By the 1890s and beyond, the detonation of fireworks by hooligans, ne'er-do-wells, and, of course, immature people, led to the formation of a group of concerned citizens called The Society for the Suppression of Unnecessary Noise. Their cause pretty much fell on deaf ears but did lead, for a while, to some restrictions—restrictions unknown to us kids in the 1950s and '60s.

On July Fourth, I used to watch my dad shoot off fireworks in our backyard when I was little and later go spread out on a blanket with family at a local country club to see big-time displays. At home, when all of our family would gather for a picnic and cookout, displays were nothing more than firecrackers, Roman candles, and maybe some benign items such as a snake

In the 1950s, some fireworks manufacturers used racist stereotypes on their packaging, such as seen on this Dixie Boy label.

or smoke bombs. As I aged, I realized that the odorous smoke bomb was a useful tool in causing an abrupt exit to any room, study hall or car. I blame it on peer pressure. Sparklers were the little kid's favorite. United Sparklers was the brand (later the Easy-Lite) we were given to run around the yard with, twirling them in circles as the flickering inferno sputtered just inches away from our bodies. Best I recall, none of the neighborhood kids ever caught on fire or lost an eye.

Roman candles, bottle rockets, aeroplanes, red phantoms (which would whistle, chase you around, and were known by another, racially-insensitive name), buzz bombs and firecrackers were all required to be set off by "responsible" adults when I was under age 7. The brand sold mostly in the South in the 1950s was Dixie Boys. We blew up a multitude of toys with those. Each flash-cracker, as they were called, came in colorful packaging called bricks. A brick contained 40 packs of 16 each with larger ones having over 15,000 inside. Lighting the entire thing would sound like a cavalry attack and was fun to watch. In five minutes we could see and hear $20 to $30 worth of my folks' money go up in flames.

Into the '60s, the Rocket brand became the most-widely purchased, along with Black Cat, which, incidentally, could explode in water. Those little powerhouses would insert nicely into a ripened tomato and, when lit and left on a homeowner's front porch just after the bell was rung, would cause collateral damage to whomever came to the door. If caught in the act, damage also occurred to one's hindquarters from the likes of a switch snapped off a small sapling just outside of our kitchen. It seems like yesterday. I still have a brick of Black Cats just waiting for the right opportunity to detonate…and to avoid capture and subsequent lashings.

As I became older, and "more responsible," a summer night with a stash of explosives was not unusual. The stash was usually left over from the Fourth and had been bought across the county line in La Vergne, Tenn., from everyone's go-to fireworks stand, Perk's on Murfreesboro Road. We bought cherry bombs, ash cans, M-80s and high-powered explosives to show off our manhood. They were called salutes, and were designed to make a loud report and, by golly, they didn't disappoint. M-80s, used by our military in the 20th century to simulate explosives and military fire, were red and about one-and-a-half inches long with a fuse sticking out of the middle and contained 3,000 milligrams of powder. The pink and red looking cherry bomb, resembling a cherry (how clever) with a fuse sticking out of it, contained five to 10 times the amount of explosives as a normal firecracker, while the silver ash can was one-and-a-half inches long and a half-inch in diameter and similar in power to the M-80. They all were deafening and came with the warning, "Do Not Hold In Hand, Light Fuse and Get away quickly." Thank goodness for that bit of information. All of these "salutes" were often misused by teens to cause disruption, panic and unnecessary destruction, and were rarely fired off with adult supervision. I admit to some disruption but no destruction, such as what happened in our elementary and high school's restrooms back in the '50s and '60s.

Cherry bombs would explode in water, which made them more attractive to misguided youths. Once lit and flushed down a commode, the ensuing eruption would often cause pipes to break and flood restrooms. The usual target: school. If the charge went off while someone was using a toilet in an adjoining facility, they would often

Sparklers were a little kid's favorite. To the best of the author's memory, no neighborhood boys or girls caught on fire or lost an eye while playing with them. (yellowbarb106, eBay)

receive a propulsion of toilet water on their derrière. I recall such an event at Woodmont Grammar school, where one of our female teachers ended up on the wrong end, literally, of a "depth charge" rumored to have been set off in the boy's restroom by kids Schulman and Seligman. Her shriek echoed down the halls and into nearby classrooms.

All schools were victimized, as were movie theaters. I cannot forget the stampede for the exits at the Green Hills Theatre in 1959 when youngster Bobby Hearn ignited several at once just as the family movie "Old Yeller" was at its most tender moment (see "Hijinks at the Green Hills Theatre" in the book "Yesterdays"). The sight of hundreds of parents and young children rushing to leave the building still brings a chuckle.

Celebrities also got in on the act. It was in 1965 when "The Who" drummer, Keith Moon, made it clear he had a fetish for cherry bombs, purchasing over 500 of them. Destroying countless numbers of toilets and amassing over $500,000 worth of damage at hotels where the band stayed on their tours, caused him to receive a lifetime ban from the Holiday Inn, Sheraton and Hilton Hotels. Quite an honor.

The most versatile of all explosives to me were the bottle rockets, and the Fruit-Loop-sized cracker balls, which, when thrown against something hard or compressed with proper force, would bang louder than the caps we used in our Roy Rogers six-shooters. Some contained more powder than others and when set off could cause a brief panic to unsuspecting citizens. Both could be detonated and transported easily, lending to rampant misuse.

In the summer of 1962, John Woodruff visited his grandfather at the Continental Apartments on West End Avenue, along with a childhood friend, whose name is withheld to protect his guilt. With too much time on their hands, they launched a barrage of bottle rockets, jettisoned from empty Double Cola and Coke bottles, at passing trucks on the busy thoroughfare down below, many of which hit their mark. Watching brake lights come on was the reward. The same kids took pockets full of cracker balls to the Belle Meade Cafeteria and indiscreetly dropped them on the brick floor, many of which went off under customers' and waiters' feet, causing vulgarities and frequent spills. The kids watched in muffled glee but were not apprehended.

On another occasion, my friend stated: "He [John] was 16 and old enough to drive, [so] we made at least a couple of trips just past the Davidson County line out to La Vergne to Perk's."

On the way back from one of those trips, a slingshot was used to fire several cracker balls at once in the direction of an unsuspecting, sweaty construction worker walking along Murfreesboro Road. At 50 miles an hour, they struck the poor soul between the shoulder blades. Believing to be shot, he collapsed to the side of the road as the youngsters sped by. I can only imagine the fear.

"It would have been funny if I'd hit him in the rear end instead of the back, but I didn't have enough sense to aim that low. I suppose the statute of limitations has run out by now."

I'll check the cold case files.

A poster warning children of the dangers of playing with firecrackers that was produced as part of the Federal Art Project in 1936 or 1937 by artist Vera Bock. (Library of Congress)

In the summer, when most of us kids played outside at night, traversing neighborhoods, meeting friends and enjoying coming-of-age things, two boys, Dave Marion and John Cooper, were doing just that one night when they showed up wielding a large, four-foot long PVC pipe filled with explosives of some kind. I believe it to be Cooper who went out to the middle of Westmont Avenue, which was my side street, crouched to one knee, and placed the "launcher" over his shoulder, resembling a WWII soldier. He said the payload would go about 50 feet and pointed the weapon eastward while several of us stood cautiously by, anticipating the show. Marion lit and dropped the ammo into the launcher, and, after a short silence, a huge fireball shot out of the tube with a thunderous BOOM. Fifty feet was a miscalculation, because the Pearson's mailbox, and the honeysuckle covering it, exploded in flames some 100 feet away across Lynnbrook Road. The best I remember, we all scattered, with no one rushing to get a hose pipe to douse the fire. Amazing how quickly

This packaging from Griff's burger bar shows their mascot, Griffy. (Steve Erikson)

kids can disappear without a sound into summer darkness.

In 1966, our Federal Government decided that too many injuries were occurring with the salutes and instituted The Child Protection Act, reducing their potency dramatically. This resulted in confiscation of the now-outlawed stuff we had as kids. An acquaintance's father was a friend of the fire chief, who knew he had a son that was into pyrotechnics. He gave the lad's father a large amount of the banned ordinance with the advice to have fun but be careful. My pal, ever the entrepreneur, decided to open up his own firework store out of his garage, capitalizing on the free explosives. His business was good until a neighborhood gal turned him in. No one was prosecuted; just a good amount of ill will was generated that has not been forgotten.

The next year, Perk's caught on fire and partially exploded. The newspaper headline read: "$250,000 Inferno…Crackling and popping sounds gave the impression that War had come to La Vergne. Roman candles and skyrockets shot out through the front door and broken windows, slamming against cars on Murfreesboro Road."

Owners Phil and Jack Perkerson said it was arson, as the culprits sawed through iron bars to get in. Rumor was they used candles for lights…smart criminals they were. All of this happened Dec. 22, 1967, just after midnight. I had an alibi—I had just gotten married and was out of town.

July 1968 was a whirlwind for my new wife as she was preparing to meet me in Honolulu for my six-month "R and R" (Rest and Recuperation) from duty in Vietnam. We were occupied with other thoughts and unaware of the happenings that took place in Green Hills on Friday, July 12. The Green Hills Theatre was showing "Camelot," billed as the most beautiful love story ever, and business was usual at J.B. Livingston's Gulf station just across the street on Hillsboro Road. At 4002 Hillsboro Road, adjacent to the station and a bottle rocket away from the theater, was everyone's favorite burger bar, Griff's (originally called Happy Burger), founded by Harold Griffin in Kansas City, Mo., and famous for its fried chocolate pies, the red-and-white striped A-frame building, and Griffy, the company logo mascot. Early that morning, Griff's was bombed. The rear of the building was damaged, but apparently not enough. On July 15, a masked marauder dropped off another bomb, this time inside the now damaged structure, and called the late-night employees "suckers" before scampering off into the night (see the news article in July 2015 issue of The Nashville Retrospect). The Gulf station, Karls' Shoes, the Village Store and Mr. Fred's Beauty Shop were all damaged. Ironically, that same day K-Mart ran a newspaper ad headlined "Bombshells." No ammunition or cheap hamburgers were part of that promotion, nor did "Mr. Fred" later advertise a reduction for "Blow-Out" hair styling.

Folks living in and around the area felt the impact, even a few miles away. Peyton Hoge was just getting home to his apartment at the Villager

Original caption from the July 15, 1968, Nashville Banner: "Damage is estimated at between $50,000 and $75,000 at Griff's Burger Bar, a Hillsboro Road drive-in restaurant destroyed early today in the second explosion in 72 hours." (Nashville Public Library, Nashville Room, photo by Bill Goodman)

Original caption from the July 15, 1968, Nashville Banner: "The rear of Griff's Burger Bar, 4002 Hillsboro Road, shows damage from an early-morning explosion, the second in three days at the drive-in restaurant. Two employes were injured." (Nashville Public Library, Nashville Room, photo by Bill Goodman)

East when the second blast occurred.

"I was opening my door and before I stepped in...boom! It shook the whole building," Hoge said.

Camping out in his garage, young Bob Taylor went over to see the carnage first hand. "It was wild," he said.

Joe Hendrick, upon observing the destruction, said: "I remember seeing mustard and ketchup packets all over Green Hills."

No word on the mayonnaise or if Griffy survived, but I highly doubt it. I guess the 11-cent crispy fries were really crispy.

Sue (Doran) Adams lived in the 4100 block of Lone Oak behind the diner: "When the first explosion occurred, it almost knocked me out of my bed, and I thought we had been attacked by the Russians."

When the second bombing happened, she said: "It woke me up, and I just said to myself, 'Oh, well, there goes Griff's again.' I turned over and went back to sleep."

It is safe to say what finished off Griff's was no "salute." It was dynamite.

Eugene Waylan, the manager, and the franchise owners, the Loyd family, had their suspicions as to the culprit (a disgruntled employee), but no arrests were ever made, although some swear they know who did it, and, no, it was not Keith Moon. It was a sad ending for some cheap hamburgers. Griff's never returned.

Since that Chinese cook blew up the evening meal 2,000 years ago, pyrotechnics have meant power, but in the wrong hands, such as what happened to Perk's and Griff's, it often led to criminal behavior. For us mostly-law-abiding kids in the 1950s and '60s, we damaged our hands, feet, eyes and worse, just to see and hear brilliant explosions. One thing was for sure, the memory of seeing folks step on cracker balls, witnessing cherry bombs obliterate plastic army men and toys, launching bottle rockets at things we shouldn't have, or just waiting with anticipation as a fuse burned down, gave us kids power. Consequences be damned. We were independent daredevils and adventurers in the danger zone, risking everything to watch something sparkle and explode. I'd probably do it all again…only if I could forego the switching.

CHAPTER 12

Back to School

> *Now you may think I'm nutty*
> *And telling you lies*
> *But I'm going out now*
> *To buy my school supplies*
> *This semester's gonna be a gas*
> *Cause school is in at last.*
> —Gary "U.S." Bonds, "School Is In" (1961)

BACK IN September of 1955, I was a seasoned scholar, a rising third-grader if you will, a veteran of the First- and Second-Grade Wars and no longer considered at the bottom of the academic food chain. I had made it even though, according to my older sister, I came home after the first day of school and told my parents: "I think one day of first grade is enough school for me." I could now cope with a little reading of "See Spot Run" and learn more good stuff about Dick and Jane. The slight boredom of summer caused me to be somewhat excited to start back to my neighborhood school.

It was a special time for kids like me, because we knew that as soon as the

Big Chief tablets like this one, said to be from the early 1950s, were used by students for writing and drawing. (Anne's Accumulations, Etsy)

Original caption from the Aug. 26, 1955, Nashville Banner: "Pencils, tablets, lunch boxes and book satchels are the proper accoutrements for the stylish first-grader. Nattily equipped to enter Julia Green's first grade as suggested by Miss Anne Dennis, center, will be from left, Katherine Sutton, daughter of Mr. and Mrs. Barrett Sutton, Kent Logan Jackson, son of Mr. and Mrs. John R. Jackson, and Arthur Graham, son of Mr. and Mrs. Edward W. Graham, Jr." (Nashville Public Library, Nashville Room, photos by John Malone)

school day ended in the afternoons, fields and open lots would be turned into practice areas for bigger boys trying to make local grade-school football squads. That meant we could watch, run around, and pretend we were playing, too. It was a time when volunteering adults would mow those areas and use contraptions that deposited lime to mark off the fields. There would be kite-flying, dogs running free, and parents lining the streets with cars. Those places were the hubs of activity for local neighborhoods.

Across the street from my house was such a spot known by locals as Herbert's Field, and at the end of the school day activity would start to pick up, with kids walking to football practice and pedaling on their bicycles, usually dressed out in their scrimmage gear. Some carried their shoulder pads across the handle bars while others came in full regalia. Boys living a mile or so away usually followed, ferried by parents in their cars. "Big kids" screeched to a halt on their bikes. Others walked down the street, their metal spikes clinking on the pavement. I can still hear the sounds in the back of my head.

Original caption from the Aug. 26, 1955, Nashville Banner: "A Flag ceremony starts the day at every public school. John Witherspoon, right, patrol leader at Parmer School, instructs a group of soon-to-be students at the school in the proper respect for the Flag. Eager listeners, from left, are: Jess Williams, daughter of Mr. and Mrs. Louis Williams, III; John B. Buchanan, son of Dr. and Mrs. Robert Buchanan, Jr.; Josephine Nelson, daughter of Mr. and Mrs. William Nelson, III; George Bullard, Jr., son of Mrs. George Bullard; Louise Dertch, daughter of Mr. and Mrs. Lawrence Dertch; Chris Fort, who holds the Flag, son of Dr. and Mrs. Garth Fort; Ray Foreman, son of Dr. and Mrs. Howard Foreman; and Joe Reeves, son of Mr. and Mrs. Joseph E. Reeves." (Nashville Public Library, Nashville Room, photos by John Malone)

After practice came the ritual procession of sweaty, future gridiron greats from Herbert's Field, crossing the street, through our gravel driveway and into our backyard to drink cold water from our hose pipe. Add to that the smell of fresh-cut grass, the sight of kids frolicking everywhere, and the entire area teeming with activity, right after the school day, made it a little easier to start school. Plus, even though we were just coming off of summer vacation, we all knew other holidays were just around the corner.

My third-grade year began Sept. 6, 1955, but prior to that day, getting school supplies and clothes were of the utmost importance.

At Woodmont, our wonderful PTA provided almost all the supplies we needed, from those fat, No. 1 pencils and the white paste (which for some kids was good enough to eat), to LePage's Mucilage glue with that sticky, crusty, rubbery tip with the slit (which nobody ate). We were well taken care of.

However, clothing was another matter, requiring moms to shift into high gear to make us young scholars presentable. Whether we played on an official grade-school football team or not, we athletic types had to have sports equipment just like the older kids. Walgreens, on Fifth at the Arcade and in the then-new Green Hills Shopping Center, had helmets reduced from $2.50 to $1.88. Their ad touted the safety factor: "The molded fiber crown is well padded for bumps," and it came with an "adjustable plastic chin strap." That should have eased every parent's mind. They also had those Big Chief tablets we all wrote in and sold loose-leaf notebook paper (75 sheets) that would fit any ring binder for only a quarter. To make certain the paper holes would not rip when placed over the rings, everyone had to have those gummed reinforcements that were sold by the box. Those circular things would stick to anything.

Lunch boxes were mandatory and essential to our learning. They told other classmates whom and what we liked. The brightly-colored and

Original caption from the Aug. 26, 1955, Nashville Banner: "Getting acquainted with their future school home is the group of children who will enter the first grade at H. G. Hill School the day after Labor Day. From left, they are: Newton Cannon, V, son of Mr. and Mrs. Newton Cannon, IV; Lynn Stevenson, daughter of Mr. and Mrs. A. Brock Stevenson, Jr.; Susan Richardson Bass, daughter of Mr. and Mrs. James O. Bass; and Estelle Tyne, daughter of Mr. and Mrs. William J. Tyne." (Nashville Public Library, Nashville Room, photos by John Malone)

This detail from a Cooper and Martin advertisement appeared in the Sept. 8, 1955, Nashville Banner. (Tennessee State Library and Archives)

metallic food containers were made by Aladdin Industries out on Murfreesboro Road right here in Nashville and were sold in department stores all over town and throughout the country. The western cowboys we saw on television had branded their own lunch boxes, so naturally that is what we wanted, plus Howdy Doody, of course. Howdy was a favorite because he, Flub-a-Dub, Mr. Bluster and cast came on television every weekday afternoon at 3:30 p.m. on Channel 4, just in time to catch all the children getting home from school.

It was a sales bonanza for clothing, shoes, food and anything that could be associated with going back to school. Cooper and Martin grocers even made corn dogs sound good with this ad for Elm Hill Tater Dogs: "The ideal snack after school" and "For a quick lunch, the Dinner on a stick." I suppose there is nothing more appealing than to have your meal impaled on a slender piece of wood—yum yum. I don't think I ever said "Gee, Mom, can I have a Tater Dog on a stick for dinner?" The only time I ever ate one of those was at the State Fair.

Even better was an in-store head-turner C&M offered: A 29-cent can of tamales billed as a "Power for a quick meal." I can't think of anything that says fresh like a can of tamales.

H.G. Hills ran this one: "Ring the Bell for Back to School Food Values," and the store offered lead pencils, two for five cents. Not sure what that had to do with food, but a good deal nonetheless. I suppose they were trying anything to prevent folks from going to the Kroger that was just opening up in the new Green Hills Shopping Center.

Many restaurants offered back-to-school deals, even the one our family used to frequent on Sundays called Bozeman's, on Murfreesboro Road. On Friday night, Aug. 26, you could get a dinner for a shocking $1. I think we passed on that one. It was probably liver and onions anyway.

Shoppers flocked to clothiers for school savings in record numbers in 1955, lured in by promotions such as what Castner Knott did in opening their "Castner's School Zone, Everything for back to school," they said. On top of that, you could pay later by using their Revolving Charge Account. They sold everyone's favorite pants, Duck Head Jeans, for $1.98, proclaiming they had "A style to please every boy in Nashville." Just up the street, Harveys Basement countered with "Back to School with Better Bargains" featuring girls' wool skirts and corduroy pedal pushers for the ladies at $2.99. I didn't know what pedal pushers were, but, by golly, they were $2.99 at Harveys. They also had boys' double-knee jeans for $1.29, which I definitely needed, because I spent the better part of childhood tearing out the knees in all my britches, plus, these things were "sanforized," had copper rivets, and were denim to boot.

On Sept. 2, Burke's Department Store, at 416 Church, pushed "Tex 'n Jeans—Favorites with

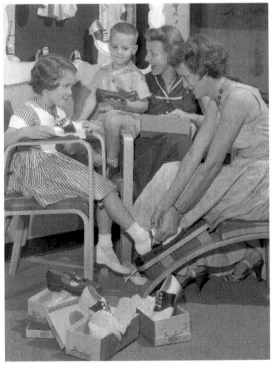

Original caption from the Aug. 26, 1955, Nashville Banner: "New shoes to start off the first grade at Woodmont School make Melissa Burrus, left and Walter R. Green, Jr., feel very grown up. Walter's mother, Mrs. Walter R. Green, watches approvingly as Mrs. Corinne Hutchison fits Melissa, the daughter of Mr. and Mrs. Byron Burrus." (Nashville Public Library, Nashville Room, photos by John Malone)

The Family Booterie and other stores are shown in this circa 1950 image of Union Street in downtown Nashville. (Metro Archives)

hard riding, rough playing, young cowhands everywhere." Hey, that was me; I was the best rough-playing cowboy in my neighborhood. Playing off of all the western themes of the day, the Robert Hall store at Seventh and McGavock had a three-day "Jamboree, Back to School Savings," touting themselves as the "Davy Crockett Headquarters." I later was told Davy would not be there—what a disappointment. National Stores had sanforized blue denim dungarees for $1.29, but if you wanted the western style it would cost $1.79. To top it all off they were "Guaranteed by Good Housekeeping." What "sanforized" meant is still open for discussion. Evidently someone named Sanford did something to the jeans fabric, but whatever it was I didn't want to know.

Over at Kress department store, girls' cotton panties went for 19 cents and 25 cents, but the rayon panties sold for up to 39 cents each. I guess the higher cost meant a bigger size. As far as the material went, I much preferred the rayon panties for the way they looked and felt, on all the girls that is.

At 212 Eighth Ave. N., Olshine's ran an ad that went like this: "A lesson in Back to School Savings. Free: A beautiful retractable ball point pen to all children accompanied by adults—absolutely nothing to buy." In addition the ad stated: "Come on in, Kids, Free Balloons and Lollipops to all." I never knew what Olshine's sold (I really thought it was shoe polish), but if a lesson was involved, count me out regardless of the lollipops and balloons.

Chester's opened Sept. 1 in the Green Hills Shopping Center, enticing folks with a back-to-school opportunity to win a 25-karat-gold raincoat worth $250: "The most fabulous raincoat that's ever been created." I am still trying to visualize it. They also sold girls' raincoats for $2.99. I could visualize that. My mother dropped off me and a couple of friends so we could also visualize "Francis in the Navy" that opened at the Tennessee Theater on Sept. 2, a Friday, as kind of a last movie before school commenced. I loved the talking mule, plus, Mom could shop while we watched.

After a summer of running through creeks and playing outside, new shoes were necessary. McClure's at 1801 21st Ave. went with this ad: "Mother, start them to school in Buster Brown Shoes that really fit." We all loved Buster Brown and his little dog Tag, whether or not the shoes fit. Family Booterie told us "Students need U.S. Keds, the Shoe of Champions" and sold another brand called Yanigans for $4.95. Not sure what those looked like, but I was accused of participating in some yanigans, or something like it, for most of my youth. They also sold the famous Red Goose shoes. Who could forget going into the store, pulling the goose's neck, and being rewarded with the Golden Egg? I recall the goose's neck being

This Olshine's advertisement appeared in the 1950s in the Nashville Banner. (Tennessee State Library and Archives)

Original caption from the Aug. 26, 1955, Nashville Banner: "Tommy Anderson, left, and his brother, Edgar Anderson, safety patrol leaders at Burton School, explain highway and bicycle safety rules to a trio of future school citizens. They are from left, Frank Thomas McCoy, III, son of Mr. and Mrs. Frank McCoy, Jr., and Mary Lee Manier, daughter of Mr. and Mrs. William R. Manier, III, who will enter the first grade at Burton, and Genevieve Lewis Steele, daughter of Mr. and Mrs. Allen M. Steele, a first grader at Robertson Academy." *(Nashville Public Library, Nashville Room, photos by John Malone)*

Original caption from the Aug. 26, 1955, Nashville Banner: "A prerequisite for entrance in the first grade of the public schools is a birth certificate. Mrs. Ames Johnson, left, of the Division of Vital Statistics of the State Department of Public Health, issues the necessary copies to Ida Hamilton Thompson Gayden, daughter of Dr. and Mrs. Hamilton Gayden, and Betty Phillips, daughter of Mr. and Mrs. Albert Phillips, who will enter the first grade at Glendale School. Mrs. Phillips, center, accompanied the children to the office in the Cordell Hull Building."

snapped off once, to the horror of all us kids. Evidently, the goose had been up to some yanigans himself in the back, because shortly thereafter, the manager came out with another Goose. It must have been the son of Red Goose. I wore the heck and the neck out of those shoes.

Even though our third-grade class at Woodmont had 30 students in 1955 (Neely's Bend fourth grade had 64 and so did H.G. Hill), all pupils seemed well-behaved, even when we were told to do the "duck-and-cover" drill and to prepare for the second round of our polio vaccine that would come within weeks. Our teacher, Mrs. Clark, was partly responsible, if for no other reason than she was the best-looking teacher in all of Woodmont. No one gave her a tough time.

Students at a New York City school in 1951 practice a "duck-and-cover" air raid drill in preparation for a possible nuclear bomb attack. (Corbis)

If you started third grade in 1955, I hope it was a good year for you whether or not you wore sanforized dungarees or ate a tater dog on a stick. All I can say is that, for me, it was some of the best of times.

CHAPTER 13

An Education in Mischief

*Don't know much about history
Don't know much biology
Don't know much about a science book
Don't know much about the French I took
Don't know much about geography
Don't know much trigonometry
Don't know much about algebra
Don't know what a slide rule is for…*
—Sam Cooke, "Wonderful World" (1960)
—Herman's Hermits, "Wonderful World" (1965)

IF YOU were in school back in the 1960s and didn't know much about all the classes you took, or how to use a slide rule, or really couldn't care less about all of it, then your classroom behavior was probably compromised. I suspect it was blamed on boredom, which was every parent's excuse, blaming their child's poor deportment on them being "very smart and not challenged enough." Some of the troublemakers fit into this category, however, most of us could not claim this crutch. A lack of interest, or just too much energy to burn during adolescence, was more like it. I was one of those kids.

Mr. Weyland Alsup was my physical-education teacher at Woodmont elementary during my first four to five years of schooling in the mid-1950s. His office was a small shed located close to our elevated playground. I became aware that there were paddles in that office, because after being told repeatedly not to throw sawdust up in the air from the area underneath the jungle gym and failing to comply with the warning, I was personally introduced to

The Woodmont School fourth-grade class of Mrs. Rose Warren in 1957. The author is in the fourth row, first kid from the left. Tamara Hicks is in front of him, first kid on the third row. Paul Clements is on the second row from the top, last kid on the right.

one of them. I had other rule infractions, so many that the paddle became my own—Mr. Alsup had my name inscribed on the handle. Quite an achievement, I thought.

Talking in class, not paying attention, or repeatedly acting out warranted either a trip to Principal Garriot's office for a paddling or, if our teacher was so inclined, writing something like "I will not talk in class" 100 times. If given a choice, I usually took the writing to save my backside. I had to do that so many times that I developed my own method; I would write "I" one hundred times first, followed by the next word and then the next and so on. I thought it would speed up the process. It didn't.

Who knows what happened to poor Jimmy Jordon when he "lost it" one day in Mrs. Rose Warren's fourth-grade class. Tamara (Hicks) Williams

Coach Solon Apple administers a paddling to Charles Biter down in the boiler room at Overton High School in 1961. (Charles Biter)

remembers that Warren "ran a tight ship…and was teaching us astronomy, for Pete's sake" when this happened.

"Everyone went into shock" said Tam.

Maybe it had to do with something that Goofus did to Gallant in the "Highlights for Children" magazine that sent Jimmy into orbit and caused him to begin throwing all his lunch money, mostly of the coin variety, into the air. Not only that but pencils and crayons were snapped and Top-Flite notebook paper got ripped to shreds and tossed about. What brought this on is not really known, but my pal Paul and I believe he had some sort of phobia against anything yellow. Kids knew this and would send him notes that, when unfolded, were nothing but yellow in color. That is our best guess. Aren't little kids understanding?

With this particular episode, it took Mrs. Warren a while to restore order and settle the youngster down. She actually dismissed class early, from our portable, so she could counsel the distraught lad. I am not sure what type of punishment he received, but he was not in our fourth-grade class picture that year, nor do I remember seeing him again. Let's hope they let him live.

Like in most elementary schools in the 1950s and '60s, radiators provided winter warmth. They were incredibly efficient, even though they often hissed and blew steam. One of the first things we learned as students was not to touch them. Most kids learned the hard way, but that mistake only happened once. Realizing how hot those iron things were, it didn't take long to figure out they had melting capabilities. Crayons and pencil erasers did not last long, quickly giving off an unpleasant odor. Mischievous children trying to melt something had to hold whatever it was in place for a period of time, often resulting in capture by the teacher. Ingenious kids figured out a better plan. Chewing gum was a no-no in school, but if you could slip it in, chew it in secret, and then stick it to the backside of the radiator, everyone in the room would be rewarded with the "odor of the day." Plus the aroma was "time released," enabling the perpetrator several minutes to take his or her respective seat.

I watched the television show "Mr. Wizard," and I knew that plastic, when subjected to extreme heat, would bubble up, melt and give off whatever smell it contained. I couldn't get away with it in the first grade, because I was too much in awe of everything. In Mrs. Sherrod's second grade you risked death for misbehaving, while in third grade, Mrs. Clark was too cute to irritate. Mrs. Warren put up with very little nonsense in fourth, but in Mrs. Johnson's fifth-grade class discipline was compromised somewhat, particularly when behaviorally-challenged Leonard Martin would act out. Classroom laughter and disruption were mainly caused by his repeated flatulent noises, made by placing his palm over his mouth while pretending to use the bathroom located in the rear of the class and then flushing the commode as if something had actually taken place. For this repeated crime, he was required to sit beside the teacher. To me this was not real punishment.

I figured I could delay class, provide a fresh classroom scent, and get away with something all at the same time. Shoot, even if caught, sitting beside Mrs. Johnson was no real punishment anyway. It would be just the thing. Plus we needed something to replace the smell of chalk-filled erasers, white paste, yellow raincoats, and those rubber, buckled galoshes sitting in our cloak room. Swell bubble gum, Teaberry, Beaman, and Juicy Fruit chewing gum were too mild. Black Jack was my choice—yuk.

Charles Biter in his 1961 school picture at Overton High School. (Charles Biter)

Before class and prior to our teacher entering our classroom, in the winter of 1958,

I chewed several pieces of the distasteful stuff, carefully stuck the glob on the backside of the steaming radiator next to the windows, and took my seat, just as Mrs. Johnson and the other kids filed in. I believe it was during or right after devotional or the Pledge of Allegiance that the pungent essence of liquorice became too invasive to ignore. Kids started commenting: "Pew," "Something stinks," and "What is that awful smell?"

Mrs. Johnson figured out pretty quickly what had happened. Cecil, our janitor, was summoned to locate and remove the bubbling gum, while most of us were allowed to step outside for some fresh air. After a minute or two of the teacher reminding us children not to bring gum to school, class resumed. My mission of delaying class was accomplished, and I was not discovered, but I let my pals know I was the perpetrator. Unfortunately, kids that age don't keep secrets. Word made its way to the main office, and I was questioned by Mr. Garriott, our stern, one-armed principal. I confessed, because I was not a liar. I received my few backside whacks from him and enjoyed a switching from Mom as well. I then went back to being a well-behaved kid, if only for a few days.

In the background is the second-story ledge at Overton High School on which Charles Biter almost became trapped, just outside of Mrs. Jean Litterer's homeroom. The picture also shows English teacher Miss. Billie Cook with some students. *(Charles Biter)*

Grade school was one thing, but high school was an entirely different animal. Classroom conduct had no limits, if you desired to push the envelope and risk the consequences. During these years, inadvisable conduct, by kids and teachers, should have been listed as part of the curriculum. It was just as much a part of the school day as reading, writing, and arithmetic.

At John Overton High, on Franklin Road in 1960, track-team members Lee Crouch and

Charlie Biter were spitting water on each other outside of the locker room after track practice when the spitting went off target.

"I chased him [Crouch] around the corner, spitting all the way," Biter recalled, "and spit on both the Assistant Principal Lucien Battle and Coach Solon Apple. Licks from the paddle in gym shorts and strap really stung."

I guess so, Charlie. Just a couple years later, Biter, showing off his track and daredevil skills and to just be "funny," decided to climb out of the second-floor window and onto the ledge of Mrs. Jean Litterer's homeroom, because she was late that spring day. The only problem was that as he sprinted along the ledge, "good friends" shut the windows on his route so he could not get back into the building.

Mrs. Jean Litterer, a teacher at Overton High School, pictured in 1964. (Charles Biter)

"I sprinted to the last window and vaulted in, only to put my knee through the glass of the lower one, just before she entered the class," Biter said. "She bought my explanation that the window was stuck and that I had to force it to close it."

Fortunately for Charles, she had experienced the same thing, too, and was sympathetic.

"I loved that woman. I dodged a big bullet," he said.

The only injury was to the knee in his torn Levi jeans. One bullet he didn't dodge involved "flipping a bird"—the obscene gesture that consists of elevating one's middle finger straight up in the air while all other fingers are turned down. He got caught in a photo taken in the Overton cafeteria that was to appear in the 1963 annual.

"I was ratted out the next spring when Mr. Hood, the photographer, told the principal," Biter said. "Mr. Battle administered the whipping."

It was just another trip down to the boiler room for backside punishment for the youngster. His parents had to be proud.

Girls misbehaved as well. Co-ed Bonnie Shields Barker, not being a fan

Teacher Portia Clark at Hillsboro High School in 1965.

of finals, decided to put socks in all the alarm bells during the May 1964 exams, interrupting all the class schedules. Ingenious. I hope she passed.

In 1961, Kay Knox and some freshmen Overton girlfriends stood outside Mr. Crawford's homeroom after lunch one day and wouldn't let him in unless he gave each of them a kiss.

"He was such a cutie," Knox said. "Unfortunately, he didn't [give us a kiss] and threatened to call our parents if we did not go in and sit down."

"Sexual harassment" was not a phrase back then, and thank goodness for that.

Those teachers with passive personalities, somewhat shy and naïve at times, often received the brunt of poor conduct. In 1964 at Hillsboro High, one such teacher, Portia Clark, could hear rock-and-roll music but could not figure out the source. Young Bobby had a way of indiscreetly irritating those in charge, and Mrs. Clark was not to be given a pass. According to a fellow classmate, a homemade transistor radio kit was placed behind a radiator with alligator clips attaching it to the frame. It seems the high-school senior knew signals could be picked up when latched on to anything metal. Once hooked up, tuning into WKDA or WMAK was easy. As the classroom giggled and did the pony in their seats, befuddled Mrs. Clark continued with her teaching duties, never to find out where the sounds came from.

That was mild compared to what later happened. She, as most instructors do, had to go into the supply closet in their room to get paper and other items for part of a day's lesson. Once, while

A transistor radio kit like this one came in handy for a school prank at Hillsoboro High in 1964.

she was doing so, a conniving boy pulled the door shut and locked her in. Uh, oh! In a few seconds students saw the knob wiggle and heard cries: "Let me out of here! Let me out of here right now!" After several minutes, a female student opened the door and released the frazzled teacher. The word is she never asked who the culprit was. All I have is the suspect's name, but on the advice of counsel, I will keep that to myself. Poor Mrs. Clark, she might as well have had a "Kick Me" sign on her back.

James Crawford conducts a shop class in 1961 at Overton High School. Former student Kay Knox remembers him as a "cutie."

On a more mellow note, another Burro used a biology book, hollowed out on the inside, to smuggle in a half pint of whiskey he bought at Mrs. Claude Mize's Southerner Liquors at 1610 Church St. I'm told he thoroughly enjoyed learning in this manner. Hey, I bet if he took the book into Mrs. Clark's class, he could really get down with that transistor radio trebling out the hits of the day. Those kids were smart and, to my knowledge, were never discovered. They became high school legends…of sorts.

At all-male high schools, such as the one I attended, misbehaving was, shall we say, a tad more aggressive.

BUILT ON A historic Civil War battle field in Franklin, Battle Ground Academy was an all-male boarding academy and college preparatory school when I attended from the late 1950s through the spring of 1965. Our vast grounds proudly displayed a cannon, complete with a pyramid stack of cannon balls, highly visible from the main highway, Columbia Pike, that bordered the front of our facility. The school annual was named, appropriately,

Battle Ground Academy in Franklin is pictured in 1964. The cannon and cannonballs in front of the main building, along with the school's name, memorialize the Civil War's Battle of Franklin in 1865.

The Cannonball, and we even had a professor named Cannon Mayes.

In 1956 no muskets were fired and General Hood was not present when Senior Walter Pyle placed one of those heavy iron projectiles back into action. Pyle, who was a big lad and dubiously honored as the "Laziest" and "Sleepiest" of his class, took one of the balls from beside the cannon and carried it to the very back of our auditorium-like study hall, and let it go. With a substantial elevation drop, from the rear to the front edge of the low stage, and with over 100 feet to build up momentum…well, you could imagine the resulting chaos. Our wonderful French teacher, Ralph Naylor, somewhat naïve and mentally absent at times, was in charge of the afternoon study hall that day but had gone out for a few minutes, leaving Freshman Richard Sinclair as "proctor in charge." Sinclair was best described as a teacher's pet, kind of an egghead and a "sweetie." All the professors loved him. He was out of his element in this case. Sub-freshman Dicky Jewel was sitting at his desk in front and witnessed the event, after becoming aware of an increasingly loud rumbling sound from way back up the aisle.

"You could hear it bang off the desks as it rolled all the way down," Jewel said. "It hit the stage, busted out some planks, and rolled under it. The laughs could be heard around the world. Naylor returned and raised hell, getting a young student to crawl under the stage to get the cannonball, all the while shouting, 'Who did this?! I'll give you all time for this action!' He was out of control."

Pyle was listed as being a senior that year but not listed as graduating. I hope it was a misprint. As for Sinclair, he was fortunate the ordinance wasn't a live round.

When young Jewel became a senior, past misbehavior, such as the cannonball incident, had a lasting impact. Mr. Naylor had not yet been institutionalized and was often the teacher most victimized. Here he was in charge of a near-capacity study hall, when Jewel devised a new way to irritate. Using fine, clear thread (that could easily be broken if about to be discovered), he strung together several of his mother's elephant Christmas bells and taped them under a desk on the opposite side of the room, "far, far, away" from where he sat. Once everyone got quiet, he pulled the thread jingling the bells. On the first pull, heads looked up, as did Naylor's. He waited and pulled again. Naylor responded loudly: "Stop that!" The rising academic waited and pulled once more to muffled laughter and looks of bewilderment

"I kept on doing this until Naylor got so upset that he jumped off the stage and headed past the walkway dividing the seventh- and eighth-graders from the high-school kids," Jewel said. "I then pulled the string so it would break, reeling it in back to my desk. He became outraged, yelling and threatening to give demerits to the entire study hall. I was

Dicky Jewel, pictured here in 1957, became a nemesis of Mr. Naylor.

Walter Pyle, shown here in his 1956 senior picture, became known at BGA for a stunt involving one of the cannonballs pictured above.

never caught, and he never found the bells. I still smile thinking about it."

After graduation in the summer of 1961, Jewel was required to repeat a sophomore English class because of an intentional credit omission by headmaster Paul Reddick. There was no love lost between those two. This class was held above the chemistry lab on the second floor of the wing on the north side of the academic building, and Naylor was the teacher.

Back then there was little air-conditioning and these classrooms had those push out windows, which on this day were open due to the extreme heat. There were many trees students scaled around our buildings, but on this occasion Jewel used one of them to hatch a plan. He took a windup clock, climbed up a pine tree just outside of the classroom windows, faced it towards the room, set the alarm to go off during class time, climbed back down, and went to summer English as normal.

"Class started, and sure enough the alarm went off," Jewel recalled. "Naylor had a fit. He leaned out of the window to grab the clock, but it was just out of his reach. He couldn't get it, so he dismissed the class. He was pissed, never finding out who did it."

I can just see the full-suited, bespectacled professor straining to grab the ringing alarm clock as all the students rolled in hysteria. This was no Norman Rockwell moment.

Not a French scholar, nor having any desire to be one, led me and other good old Southern, English-speaking kids to find ways to make our required foreign language course more "entertaining." It was a few years later and good old Mr. Naylor, or "Goober," as he was affectionately known, was the expert instructor in charge. His past had preceded him, being best described as a man who was "not quite with it." One of his routine quirks was to go to the rear of his second-floor classroom, open up the large window, spit onto the lawn down below, and then close the window. Harassing students once opened the window prior to his arrival, and Mr. Naylor, not deviating from his habit, closed the window and spit directly on the glass and then said, "Some of you guys think you are smart."

That was a real eye-opener, but pales to the fright that Mrs. E.C. Duke, our public-speaking teacher, received when she opened up her supply closet. There was Goober. With a shriek, she asked: "What are you doing in there?" His response: "Everyone's got to be somewhere." Holy smokes.

Back in 1964, a couple of us scholars decided to hide Naylor's French book just before class began. Several professors lived on Everbright Avenue across from our campus and would only have to walk a few hundred feet or so to start their school day. Naylor was one of those. He kept his book, much like a Bible to him, in plain view on the front of his desk, just inviting someone to mess with it. On this particular day, that is exactly what happened. We hid his book just before he made his way up the stairs and into the classroom. Taking a seat, he began to shuffle around his desk looking for the missing French textbook. He opened drawers, double-checked the publications stacked in front of him, and even opened his briefcase twice. Exasperated, he mumbled to us all: "I must have left my book at home. Keep your seats and I will return shortly."

French teacher Ralph Naylor, shown in 1960, was known for saying to BGA students, "Some of you guys think you are pretty smart." He was the butt of many pranks.

BGA students in study hall are shown launching, and dodging, a spitball in 1965.

As soon as he made his way down the steps there was laughter all around. Now to determine what to do with the book. It was decided to put it back on his desk, right in front where he had looked extensively before. As an added bonus, some of us decided to balance another book above the tall door between the top ledge and the transom above it, so that when he pushed the door open, the book would fall directly on top of him. Cruelty has no bounds. Once done, we all sat quietly in our seats, waiting to hear him start back up the steps. Here he came, some 15 minutes later, as we waited in anticipation. "Goober" pushed opened the tall door and the book fell, careening off his nose and knocking his glasses off. His reply: "That was cute."

Then he sat down, began rummaging around again, and spotted his elusive French II book standing upright in front of him on his desk. His comment: "Here it is. It was here all the time." We buried our heads in our arms.

In that same class during translation time, a period where each student would speak into a microphone in French from a certain chapter in the book, some agitator came up with the idea to pass an invisible "bomb" from one person to the next and see what would happen. With the entire 20 or so kids in on the stunt, the non-existent package began its journey on the first row.

Each kid flipped both palms up, as if cradling something, and would turn to the next kid beside him and pretend to hand it off. Mr. Naylor first noticed this movement as it progressed midway down the front row, peering over his spectacles to try to figure out what was taking place. By the time the "bomb" made its way to the third row, Naylor had had enough. Just as it was passed to aspiring French linguist Billy Adair, there came the emphatic and surprising statement: "Put that thing down."

Young Adair was caught…with nothing in his hands. To oblige Naylor, he acted like he placed it on his desk. I am not sure what the demerit description would have been, but it probably would have been something like two demerits for passing an invisible object during French class. Adair said he never received time. Lord help us all.

> *Who's always writing on the wall?*
> *Who's always goofing in the hall?*
> *Who's always throwing spitballs?*
> *He's gonna get caught*
> *Just you wait and see*
> —"Charlie Brown," The Coasters (1959)

If a student or students wanted to try "to get away with something," launching spit wads and spitballs was not recommended. These saliva-laden spheres were usually thrown, but on occasions with no adult in sight they could be launched in Medieval fashion using a homemade catapult or a sling, manned by several high-school miscreants. They were often the size of baseballs, manufactured by chewing several pieces of loose-leaf notebook paper in one's mouth, all at one time. When hitting their target, they left a large splattering of evidence on classroom walls and windows, as well as on the backsides of targeted underclassmen. Apprehension of the culprits usually occurred when those underclass victims, pressured by teachers, ratted them out. Demerits for such actions were substantial. Upwards of 10 was the norm. You only got five for no homework.

A much safer and less detectable method of launching something, other than spitballs, was to use a thick rubber band stretched between the thumb and forefinger in the form of a "V" (kind of like a slingshot), then load it with a silver BB or pellet from a Daisy air rifle. An accomplished marksman could be upwards of 100 feet away, say in the back of the study hall, and fire those tiny projectiles, striking the venetian blinds that covered the expansive windows behind the main desk, just beyond where the monitor sat on the stage way down front. Those pellets were unseen by the naked eye and left hard-to-find evidence, unlike those white, moisture-laden spitballs. When those silver spheres hit, they made a loud bang always befuddling whomever the professor in charge was at the time. Teachers would always look behind them. Those immature students who continually disrupted study halls should be ashamed, whoever they were. I can tell you this: in 1963 silver was only $1.29 an ounce. I got my money's worth.

Spitballs were one thing, but draining the liquid out of all the cola bottles in the Coke machine was something else. In the basement of the old dormitory, there was a Coca Cola machine, the kind where the bottles were stacked on top of each other, in little individual compartments, accessible by opening a long glass door, but only after depositing 10 cents.

Back in the late 1950s, some of the boarding students figured they could pop the tops off those Orange Crushes, Nehi's, Coke and those delicious Brownie Chocolate drinks and get free sodas just by using a straw to suck out the good stuff. When "Bonehead," an unflattering term for our headmaster, Major Paul Reddick, found out he was furious. I wonder why? He called all dormitory students thieves and declared all would receive

Pictured in the 1964 Battle Ground Academy annual, student Johnny Nicholson is shown stealing the bell from the study-hall desk.

100 demerits. The kids who got caught spent a month of Saturdays in demerit hall and had to miss out on watching "Sky King," "Tennessee Tuexdo," "Quick Draw McGraw" and "The Adventures of Rocky and Bullwinkle," to name just a few. That was the real punishment. Questionable acts of dorm students would fill up a library. I think I will save that topic for another day.

Yes, some students continually irritated the teachers, but I suppose that was all part of the maturing process. It took some of us several years to mature, while others never did. Some of our teachers, sensing proper behavior was taking longer than expected, took matters into their own hands and turned the tables on us. You know, pain and suffering definitely sped up the process.

> *Ding, A-Ding Ding Ding, Ding Ding,*
>   *Ding.*
> *Dong, A-Dong Dong Dong, Dong,*
>   *Dong, Dong.*
> *Whispering Bells, Loud and Clear,*
>   *our Sweet Chimes, Glad to Hear…*
> —The Del-Vikings, "Whispering Bells" (1957)

Bells were synonymous with grammar schools and high schools for as long as I attended, from 1954 to 1965. Those jingly Christmas bells that irritated Mr. Naylor were an exception. Nonetheless, bells were part of the learning process. They ranged in size from the large Liberty-like bells on top of school houses to the wall-mounted, change-of-class and school-day-ending bell (the kind stuffed with a sock by an Overton High coed in 1964), to the little nickel-plated, hand-sized ones that sat on business reception counters and on school teachers' desks. In earlier years those ringers had a handle attached to the top. They were also prevalent in drug stores, hotels and medical offices. Those ringers used in school settings signaled students that it was time to pay attention, straighten up, shut up, and come to order. They were definitely "Loud and Clear," but I am not so sure we were "Glad to Hear" them.

At Battle Ground Academy, almost every instructor had one on their desk. It was a staple of the professor in charge of study hall, always present and

Geoff Winningham, alleged bell-swiper, was implicated by evidence later found by his brother David, who disposed of the box of bells found in a closet.

clearly visible on the long table that sat on the stage. If the class became too loud, the teacher in charge would tap the little nodule on the top to produce a "ding" sound audible to all kids in the vicinity. It also meant "cool it" and "quiet down or else." Meek substitute proctors and teachers just kept tapping the bell, usually achieving little response. To a lot of us, it was like "crying wolf" over and over. We ignored the ring.

It was back in the 1960–1961 school year that those little silver desktop bells began vanishing, "at an alarming rate," according to Bert Phillips, a senior at the time. Many years ago he told David Winningham, whose brother Geoff was deemed "Most Dependable" and was president of Phillips' class, that after a few months of dwindling bells, Headmaster Major Paul Redick summoned the entire student body into study hall to discuss the matter. Winningham relates the story from Phillips:

"Redick, after asking the culprit to come forward and receiving no response, proceeded to walk the aisles and ask each student, one by one, if they knew anything about it. However, when he came to me, Bill Redick [the headmaster's son], and Geoff, he skipped over us."

No way his own son and especially the "Most Dependable" president of the senior class would be involved in such thievery. This turned out to be poor detective work. Winningham said that in 1967, right after his marriage, he began cleaning out a closet in his old home. As Jim Nabors, alias Gomer Pyle, used to say in the television show "Gomer Pyle, USMC": "Surprise, surprise, surprise."

"Stuck deep in the back of the top shelf was a sizable cardboard box filled with bells," Winningham said. "Having followed Geoff to BGA, I had heard the reports of the 'disappearing bells' and the study hall inquisition. I fell out laughing upon my discovery."

Unfortunately, those ringers were all thrown away. Nothing like destroying evidence to preserve a brother's Most Dependable reputation.

Only two years later, in the 1963–1964 school year, those desktop ringers continued to be a highly-prized item. Though detested by most every student as symbols of a teacher's disciplinary control over the unruly behavior of misguided teens, the capture of a bell was seen as a trophy of sorts, similar in stature to a wild beast of the African continent seen on the big-game hunting television show "Mutual of Omaha's Wild Kingdom," starring Marlin Perkins. Only this time around, bell theft was not as pronounced as during Geoff Winningham's reign. Nonetheless, swiping one from the study hall desk, without being detected, was still practiced.

Fortunately, pictures that appear in school annuals are often shot months prior to publication and therefore are not immediately visible to students and teachers alike. For instance, there is little information on the consequences suffered by Johnny Nicholson Jr., who was photographed in the act of pilfering the study hall bell in 1963. Nicholson's senior quote stated: "He that climbs the tall tree, has won right to the fruit." I guess the stage was the tree and the bell was the fruit. My belief is that the picture went undetected by our headmaster, otherwise there would have been some ringing-in-the-ears, double-digit demerits, and a delayed graduation ceremony heaped upon the young scholar.

A similar fate could have befallen my classmate Mick McCoy, who

There are quite a few antics going on in the author's 1964 junior class photo, from costumes to hats to simply wearing one's clothes backwards. But one serious offense that apparently avoided detection can be seen in the lower left-hand corner (Hint: Hand gestures).

140   Best of Times

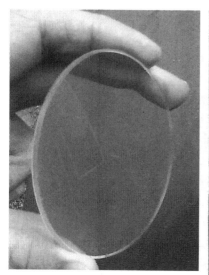

Above is the author's magnifying glass which, when spun on a desktop, creates a "flying saucer" sound effect, like those featured on the records above and the 1956 movie "Earth vs. The Flying Saucers" (right)

indiscreetly displayed a sleight of hand in our 1964 junior class photo, not in the swiping of bells but in the "shooting of birds." When McCoy was asked if he received any demerits for his actions, he replied: "I don't think so, but, hell, I got so many demerits I don't really remember." Hopefully the statute of limitations has run out on both. Kudos to the class photographer for concealing the evidence until publication time.

The sound of bells was one thing; UFOs were quite another. It was during my sophomore year, in 1962–1963, that a British musical group called the Tornados came out with a No. 1 hit instrumental entitled "Telstar." They had capitalized musically on the space race, started by the Russians when they launched a satellite called Sputnik in 1957. The song had eerie parts at the beginning and end that sounded a lot like one of those flying saucers we all saw at theaters and in science-fiction gems like "Earth vs. The Flying Saucers" in 1956. Novelty recording artists Buchanan and Goodman got on the band wagon, too, that same year with the 45-rpm record "The Flying Saucer" and followed it the next year with "Flying Saucer the 2nd," which had that outer-space noise at the end. (I spent my money well in those days, because I bought both of those classics down at Buckley's).

All of this alien stuff and science-fiction films were prevalent at the time and hung out in the far reaches of our precious little minds. Well, somewhere I had found a convex magnifying glass that resembled one of those saucers, and, out of boredom, I happened to twist it like a top on my desk one day in study hall, while either serving off demerits or spending time on the non-privilege list. I forget which one. (I am sorry to say that I was a regular attendee of both). The resulting sound emulated one of those crafts coming in for a landing. The wooden desks we had amplified the whirring sound so much that it could be heard all the way up to the front of the auditorium.

Realizing I had a real "conversation piece" on my hands, I decided to see what the reaction would be if I continued to spin it. In order to avoid detection, I had to conceal it behind my "Word Wealth" and algebra books, which I had stacked up on the front part of my desk. It was hard to believe, but after a couple of more spins, some eighth-graders rose up out of their seats to look out of the windows. Good gracious. Attack of the flying saucers was now a reality. Only after repeating this maneuver several times did the kids figure out where the landing zone was. I don't recall the teacher, but—and I hate to say it—I believe it to be Mr. Naylor, who was in charge of study hall that day.

The author's "Flying Saucer" 45-rpm records from the '50s.

Professor Boardman Stewart and the BGA "Classroom Quizbuster" team in 1965.

He, too, was temporarily perplexed, finally saying, after removing his specs, "Who or whatever that is had better stop soon, or someone is going to get plenty of time." "Time" was another word for demerits. I determined that it was in my best interest to ground further extraterrestrial operations. I have kept that UFO object all these years and recently re-launched it. My dog left the room. It sounds as good as ever. Oh, the memories.

Receiving demerits, in moderation, was considered by some to be a small badge of honor. Receiving them in large quantities—not so much. The demerit list of honorees was not a secretive one, either. Each week in an all-school assembly, the recipients were duly noted, alphabetically and verbally, from the stage podium in a ceremonious fashion, often sadistically bellowed out by Boardman Stewart, the dignified English-history instructor and coach of our most brilliantly-minded scholars on the local television program "Fidelity's Classroom Quizbusters." (Unfortunately, I did not dress out for that team, even though I busted many a quiz).

Stewart seemed to take great pride in announcing each student's name and number of demerits. He followed the reading with a brief pause after which he would cite the infraction with emphatic tones, all the while sporting a slight grin. Of course, those in attendance would agitate after each name was called. For instance: "Eddy Woodard, ten demerits...VULGARITY." Followed by mass laughter.

One particular reading was especially noteworthy to me, the consequence of a lunch-time incident that occurred in 1963. In our dining hall, six to eight students would sit at a long table, most often headed up by one of our teachers. Earlier that week I had been assessed "time" by Jimmy Gentry, who was the professor at the head of my table this particular day, for something like flicking a piece of fried okra during lunch at a fellow basketball player in the cafeteria. Mind you, it was in retaliation for being hit with some smallish vegetable, resembling a butter bean, thrown only seconds earlier. At the assembly reading, Mr. Stewart began scrolling down the list alphabetically. I awaited, with regretful anticipation, for my name to be announced. Guess what? Stewart went right through the H's without mentioning my name. I gave a muffled "Yes," believing Mr. Gentry had failed to report my flinging of the okra. Well, sir, as Stewart got to the end of the alphabet, he folded up his list, started to leave the podium and abruptly turned back around and gleefully bellowed this out: "And Mr. Henderson, five demerits... FOR THROWING FOOD." The study hall erupted as I slumped down below my desk. Stewart could have cited this profound quote from one of his English-history homework assignments: "The latter end of joy is woe"—Geoffrey Chaucer, "The Canterbury Tales." He wasn't that sadistic. I must say that Mr. Stewart did have a good heart, because he allowed me to go to his home, out on the Lewisburg Pike, and assist him and his

A typical student assembly at BGA in 1965. Among other things, the names of students receiving demerits were read aloud.

lovely wife Lillian in preparing for a weekend soiree by polishing door knobs, amongst other chores, for the better part of two hours, thus commuting my sentence to time served. I never threw any more okra.

Acting out, general misconduct, and the poor behavior of a kid might get him by with only receiving demerits…usually. But if your actions were detected by a couple of our teachers in particular…well, let us just say demerits were not all the punishment you incurred. You'd best cover up.

Mairzy doatz and dozy doats
And liddle lamzy divey
A kiddley divey, too,
Wouldn't you?
—The Merry Macs (1944)

AT BATTLE Ground Academy, a couple of teachers, when they caught kids doing things they were not supposed to do, awarded the offending students with, not only demerits, but physical punishments as well. One of the teachers was our much-celebrated algebra instructor, Carl "Goat" Smithson. Seems that he had come by that nickname from his tenacious blocking while a member of the Trevecca College football team. Word was he would knock opposing linemen out of the way by head-butting them. I don't doubt it a bit. His classroom "corrections" were also of legendary status, often involving the head area. More on that later.

Capitalizing on our school's rural location in Franklin, with its accompanying farm land, livestock and open spaces, two students—a Cuban boarder named Pedro Paz and his best pal and local kid Mike Hudgins—came up with a plan that would forever ingrain Smithson's nickname in school lore. They would bring a real goat to school. Oh, me.

It was during the 1955–1956 school year that Hudgins and Paz came up with the idea for their mischievous adventure to "borrow" a goat. Back then, boarding students were required to be in study hall nightly from 7 to 9 p.m., and Hudgins, due to some academic deficiencies, was made to be in attendance as well, even though not a boarding student. He only lived a block or two away on Adams Street, so for him it was not that big of a deal to cross Columbia Pike, hop over one of the little three-foot maple trees on Battle Ground's front lawn, and enter the main building.

He and Pedro knew of a cute little goat, owned by a black gentleman, that grazed on a light-weight chain in an open field on Academy Street, just across from the then-new George I. Briggs Gymnasium at the end of campus. After study hall had ended, the plan was put in motion. It was after 10 p.m., and Smithson's room was upstairs on the second floor.

Pictured in the 1955 Battle Ground Academy annual, algebra teacher Carl "Goat" Smithson is pranked with a real goat (the two student culprits, in jackets, look on).

"Once we removed the goat from his chain," Hudgins recalled, "we gently walked it to Mr. Smithson's classroom. With the goat safely retained in Mr. Smithson's classroom, we closed the door and went our own ways."

A brief translation of the No. 1 hit, "Mairzy Doats" novelty song's third line: "A kiddley divey, too" means a kid (a young goat), will eat ivy, too. This goat did more than eat ivy.

You can imagine the chaos a creature would create by being locked up in a confined area all night, particularly with lots of things to munch on. As expected, all hell broke loose the next day.

"Coming into the administration building the next morning," Hudgins said, "I could hardly get up the steps due to the crowd of students laughing and giggling as they peered in Smithson's classroom. I recall him standing in the middle of the doorway, leading into his room, looking as if he had just swallowed a hot stove and, to the best of my memory, was blaming the

BGA student Mike Hudgins confessed to the 1955 goat incident but to no avail.

visiting goat on everyone he saw. Glancing into his room, I could see the goat had eaten each and every one of his fancy geometric figures [Smithson] had made in graduate school and had so carefully placed on his short book shelves. In return, the goat had left a neat pile of little round goat poop."

I can only imagine that the aroma left behind was not on the pleasant side. Hudgins, now feeling a bit of guilt that some other student would be blamed, tried to own-up to the crime. After repeated confessions, all he got from Mr. Smithson was "No, Mike, you are not responsible for this. You are not smart enough."

Wow, a reprieve and a blow to the ego. About that time, Headmaster Paul Redick showed up and looked into the room.

"I made my way through all my fellow students and said to Mr. Redick that Mr. Smithson is blaming everyone he lays eyes on," Hudgins said. "Pedro and I brought the goat to his room late last night, and all he can say in return is, 'No, Mike, you're not smart enough.' Mr. Redick looked at me with a little grin on his face and said, 'Mike, don't worry about it too much.'"

Pedro Paz, a boarding student at BGA in 1955, was also implicated in the goat prank.

Whoa. Apparently Redick enjoyed Smithson's goat follies.

After things cooled off, Hudgins and Paz walked the goat back "to his lush green field and his light-weight chain. It was all over." As it turns out, this was the second visit by the goat. Pedro and Mike, a couple of years earlier, had "borrowed" the creature and took it to morning assembly.

"The goat walked right in as if visiting friends and relatives," Hudgins said.

He claimed the goat seemed to enjoy the publicity and never complained, unlike Mr.

Smithson, the other goat. No word on how many demerits were passed out or who cleaned up the mess, but it has been reported that our maintenance man—Otis Stutts, I believe—along with some underclassmen, were seen with buckets and mops entering Smithson's room shortly thereafter. It is further noted that Hudgins and Paz both were allowed to graduate on time. That, in itself, remains a mystery to me. Who knows what happened to the real goat.

Fast forward several years to 1964, when, at sum-

Another goat prank played on Smithson, this one in 1962.

mer's end, in his second-floor, non-air-conditioned classroom, Smithson, with the nickname "Goat" now firmly attached, did what he was famous for: He enacted sadistic rituals on misbehaving students. On this particular mid-afternoon in Algebra II class, in order to keep the breeze moving in the 80-degree heat, he had placed a six-foot tall, upright fan in the center of the room. Its blades were shielded only by a few pieces of steel and blew full blast, pointing slightly upward, in order to disseminate the air around the walls. Us students were in rows mostly forward of its placement so as to benefit from the cooling breeze.

I was sitting just towards the back row, in front, and slightly off to the left side of the churning fan, while fellow classmate Hayes was behind and over to the right side. As a struggling kid in that class, and with a pop quiz in progress, I made a decision, based on the monotonous hum of the fan and the silence of conscientious classmates taking the test, that the atmosphere of the room needed to be adjusted. Armed with several pieces of broken Crayola white chalk I had pocketed from doing problems on the blackboard, I discreetly leaned back just behind the fan as if stretching and flicked a piece into the spinning blades. The resulting sound closely resembled that of someone stepping on a cat's tail. Mr. Smithson looked up and then continued on doing paperwork, as the other kids continued with the exam. This did nothing to alter the setting, so after a brief pause of 20 to 30 seconds, I once again leaned back and this time tossed an arsenal of full pieces into the whirring machine. Once the chalk entered the rear and came in contact with the blades, they were pulverized into small, microscopic bits and jettisoned out the front at the speed of sound, which, at this time, sounded more like a buzz saw slicing a two-by-four in half. Several kids in front ducked while the remainder of the pieces made loud noises on the black board and on Smithson's desk some 20 feet away at the front of the classroom. Off came his glasses. He looked around and then shouted "Hayes, come down front."

Hayes was shocked and professed his innocence as he slowly meandered to the front of the room amidst oohs and aahs by fellow students who knew what was coming. Repeated claims of "Mr. Smithson, I didn't do anything" were to no avail. Smithson, who was known to have demerit-laden scholars bust rocks, pick weeds and do other assorted labor activities on Saturdays at his farm, affectionately called Rock-A-Rosa, in an effort to serve off their time at a faster pace, also had a reputation for smacking delinquents with rulers or a small jigsaw blade. Hayes knew this, but what could he do? Smithson commanded the pleading student to get on his knees by the teacher's desk. Once Hayes knelt down, our esteemed algebra instructor proceeded to do what he also usually did to me and other kids not behaving properly. He "picked cotton." What is that, you

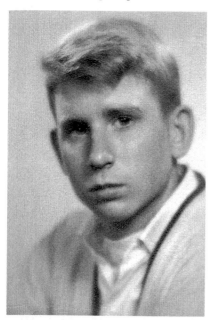

The author is shown in his 1964 BGA class photo, the year the chalk hit the fan.

Smithson applies his unique form of discipline to a student by pulling out small clumps of hair, a punishment known as "pickin' cotton."

say? Well, it entailed bowing your head while Goat pulled your hair until you learned your lesson. When picked correctly, the clump of hair extracted from our scalps resembled that of a freshly picked cotton ball. Picture an episode of "The Three Stooges" in which Moe Howard yanks out Larry Fine's curly locks. Ouch. Unfortunately for Hayes, the lesson he learned was that life was not fair. I, who had often been summoned to submit to a palm-thrashing with the jigsaw blade and to have my cotton picked with the call of "Thomas, you redheaded peckerwood, come down front," quite enjoyed watching someone else take the punishment for a change, even if it wasn't justified. I failed to implicate myself.

What wasn't justified, and what has been rumored for many years, was my supposed banishment from algebra class one winter's day in 1963, for what has best been described as "academic disruption." This was according to classmate Ed Graham. The story goes that I was kicked out of class and forced to go

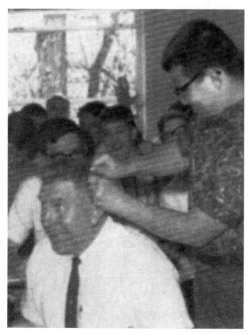

Student Steve Plonka was allowed some cotton-pickin' revenge by Smithson in 1964.

outside and stand on the snow-covered ground in freezing conditions, with no coat, gloves, or appropriate cold-weather gear for the remainder of our 45-minute period. Graham recalls I chucked snowballs at the window for upwards of 15 minutes, shouting, "It's cold out here!" He swears by the story, although, in my recollection, I believe it was fellow student Jimmy Short who spent that algebra class outside. In my head I can still visualize Short shivering outside in the cold. The mind is a wonderful thing. It wasn't me.

It must be said that Mr. Smithson was a good sport. He endured the goat coming to algebra class in 1955 and was pictured smiling while holding onto the leash. He also suffered through the discovery of a mounted goat head that some urchin had installed on his classroom wall in 1962. So in 1965, after years of revenge inflicting various forms of physical abuse to misbehaving students, he allowed my fellow classmate, pudgy boarding student Steven Plonka, to pluck cotton from his red head while another kid captured the event with a photograph. This type of thing endeared him to many students. I am not saying Hayes was one of them, though.

Too bad Goat didn't keep the four-legged animal. It could have alleviated some work for demerit burdened students at his famed Rock-a-Rosa farm. Plus, had he made the creature part of his classroom, it would have enabled him to delegate the punishment of picking cotton to the real goat. I was told, in fact, that goats eat cottonseed. Chomping teenagers' hair might have crossed the line. However, at BGA back then, I kind of doubt it.

An Education in Mischief

Same thing every day, gettin'
 up, goin' to school
No need for me to complain,
 my objection's overruled, ahh!
Too much monkey business,
 too much monkey business
Too much monkey business
 for me to be involved in
—Chuck Berry, "Too Much Monkey Business" (1956)

THERE WAS a whole lot of monkey business going on at my school, and, I hate to say it, but I was involved with some of it. I guess I "got in with the wrong crowd of characters."

Of course, it wasn't limited to only the students. We definitely had our cast of character instructors, some with well-known nicknames, who taught us life's lessons. There was: Bob Knight ("Bub Nut"); Don Patterson ("Dog"); Tony Cobb, who taught Latin and English and was called many things, all politically incorrect by today's standards (he was also the son of WSM

Teacher John Bragg was pictured in the 1963 annual with the caption, "Develop a two page theme," which was a weekly assignment.

personality David Cobb, who coined the term "Music City, USA"); Mr. Naylor (affectionately called "Goober") with his infamous sayings of "Everybody has to be somewhere" and "Some of you guys…" and "Immediately if not sooner"; "Goat" Smithson and his "cotton-picking" methods; Headmaster Major Paul Reddick (referred to as "Bull" and "Bonehead," behind his back, of course), whose stories defied belief; "Honey" J.B. Akin, who was extremely frugal; and Mr. John Bragg ("Chin"), our English professor and a World War II combat veteran who personally helped me acquire admission to an accredited college and thereby continued our school's senior class record of 100-percent admissions to universities. His "Word wealth" "musical chairs" ingrained in me an expanded knowledge of the English language. Fortunately, records were not kept on how long we stayed in our respective universities.

Those unforgettable professors, during my tenure, are just a few that come to mind.

Then there was one of our most respected and admired professors, Mr. Daly Thompson, himself a 1910 Battle Ground Academy graduate, reverently labeled by us kids as "Monk" (I suspect for his ape-like appearance), and also "Creeping Jesus." The latter term came from his ability to move from the front of our enormous study hall all the way to the back without hardly making a sound. Thompson always wore a full three-piece suit, often times with tennis shoes, which enabled his movements to be virtually inaudible when stalking an out-of-line student. Not sure if they were Keds, Red Ball Jets, Converse or Buster Brown's. I tried not to get that close.

George Leonard was caught by "Monk" sipping a soft drink in demerit hall and avoided physical punishment by running out of the building.

One Friday afternoon in 1964, fellow Senior George Leonard was sneaking an occasional sip or two from a Dr. Pepper soft drink in demerit hall. I know because I saw the 10, 2, and 4 numbers on the bottle, which was the slogan at the time. This was a definite no-no. There was no drinking or eating allowed. If caught, one could bank on a minimum of five

Battle Ground Academy teacher Daly Thompson is shown in study hall (above) and at his desk (below) in 1962. The subject of a few pranks, he was known for keeping his word and holding students accountable for their actions. In the top picture, from the 1962 annual, Thompson is pointing and correcting some misbehavior. The picture was mockingly captioned, "Uhhhhh...," a reference to his trademark saying, "Uhhhhh, son, don't make me have to come to ya."

demerits and a possible thrashing, particularly if witnessed by Mr. Thompson. Peering over the top of his glasses at precisely the right time, Thompson spied George (nicknamed "Sneaky Moose"), who was at his desk in the last row, just as he turned the bottle up to his lips for a quick swig. Monk yelled out, "George, is that you, son?" To which George replied, "No, sir, not me." With that Mr. Thompson, full suit, tennis shoes and all, got up from the long table on the stage and slowly began his ascent up the far aisle, obviously en route to George on the opposite side. The senior had seen

Mr. Thompson come up behind underclassman Perry Shields, a year or so earlier, and repeatedly smack him upside his head for reading unauthorized material shielded in a text book. I, too, had witnessed that thrashing. It was a frightening sight, to say the least. George was well aware what was going to take place. As Thompson started down the last aisle where George was sitting, the cola-drinking lad turned around and quickly uttered: "Mr. Thompson, if you are going to hit me, I'm going to get up and get out." Not hesitating as Monk continued his approach, George grabbed all his books, jacket and Dr. Pepper and scurried down the aisle, blistering it through the swinging doors, and escaped to parts unknown. More demerits ensued, but at least an aggravated assault was averted. No one wanted to see a Monk abuse a Moose.

One of the finest Latin instructors in the state, Thompson was widely respected by his peers and loved by his students. So much so that our school annual was dedicated to him in 1964. He was a man that also greatly admired the famed Roman emperor Julius Caesar. "Admired" was a real understatement—more like "idolized."

It was in a summer-school session in 1964 when Monk noticed a note being passed from one student to another in his class. Note-passing was not part of the curriculum, so he pushed his glasses to the front of his nose and asked for it to be brought up front. After getting several excuses as to why the note was insignificant and therefore not necessary for him to view, he became irritated and finally demanded it, saying: "Uhhh…son, don't make me have to come to ya" (a famous saying of the professor). No one wanted Mr. Thompson to "come to ya," for if he did, you would receive a flogging of the highest order. Sophomore David Bland, knowing fellow classmate Mark Rogers had a dog, a boxer named Caesar, had scribbled out an unflattering remark on a piece of paper with regards to the pooch, so unflattering that he knew if Mr. Thompson saw it, he would be in big trouble. No matter, Monk insisted the note be handed over. As Thompson opened it, his face became beet-red while his demeanor rose to Level 10, doubly so because of his love of Julius Caesar. Not knowing the derogatory script was meant for a canine, he interpreted it as a heinous slam on the great emperor. Bland was ejected and left class before he was personally extricated. As I remember, he was awarded

Caesar, a boxer dog, was the subject of a misunderstanding with Mr. Thompson. Caesar is pictured with owners Mike, Patty and Mark Rogers in 1955.

double-digit demerits for his blasphemous slander and issued a severe reprimand from the administration. The note simply said: "Caesar eats shit." His plea of "it was about a dog" was barking up the wrong tree.

It wasn't a dog, but a bird that got Monk stirred up that same year. Between the seventh, eighth and last period of the day, when the bell rang, it was always bedlam. Students exited our auditorium through large swinging double doors in a mass, as other kids came in for their final period study hall. Everyone was winding down and relieved to have another day of learning come to an end. At this point no teacher was in charge, as they too moved out of the second-floor area. For a brief time, there was no control or supervision. On this particular afternoon, through those swinging doors, entered our monitor for the final session, Mr. Thompson. As usual, he was clad in a three-piece suit, rimmed glasses, tennis shoes and all. It was during this chaos that some agitators let loose with a bevy of exotic bird calls, similar to the kinds those Piedmont Bird Callers would eventually emit in 1976 on "The Tonight Show" with Johnny Carson. However, these were not quite as refined and were more like what you would hear from the soundtrack of the 1950s television show

Teacher J.B. Akin is shown in the 1964 annual with the caption, "N-o-o-o-o boys! That would cost three times as much," which pokes fun at his frugal reputation.

"Ramar of the Jungle"—primitive at best. These "calls" would continue for as long as it took Thompson to make his way up to the monitor's table up on the stage. After several continuous weeks of this, one Friday Thompson took his customary seat at the long desk, tapped the ever present bell, and, with the study hall now silent, uttered loudly with a sly smile: "If I ever catch that bird, I am going to choke him." We knew he wasn't fooling around.

Mr. Thompson was a man of his word and held every student accountable for his actions. If you were supposed to stay after school to serve off the demerits you had accumulated, you stayed after school—period. A case in point involved a beleaguered sophomore student named John "Mooey" Mallernee. One Friday afternoon as the final bell rang and those kids who had committed offenses during the week prepared for a couple of hours of study hall, Mallernee, with myself alongside, approached Monk with a sad, pleading question. It went like this: "Mr. Thompson," Mallernee said, "the Franklin Road bus is getting ready to leave, and if I don't get on it, I will not have a way to get home except to call my parents or hitchhike. If that happens, I will be in big trouble when I get home. Can I please serve off my time next week?"

Well, sir, Thompson broke into this huge grin, leading Mallernee to believe a positive response was coming. He removed his glasses and said in his typical slow, toneful, defining voice, "Uhhh, son...I don't think so."

Mallernee dejectedly shrugged his shoulders but was humored by the inflective remark. I, on the other hand, immediately turned away in muffled laughter. Poor John had to hitchhike home. Mr. Thompson, true to his reputation, held the youngster accountable, regardless of the bus schedule. And one other thing, Mr. Thompson never caught those bird-calling students. Fortunately for them, they graduated and flew away, never to be choked to death. My wife and kids are thankful for that.

School misbehavior, back in the 1950s and '60s at my alma mater, at institutions like it, and at most public schools, usually resulted in some kind of corporal punishment, to be administered both there and at home. We expected it. It generally had a lasting impact. "I better not do that again" was the resulting thought. The words that Theodore "Beaver" Cleaver's friend Larry said to him in an episode of "Leave it to Beaver"—"Gee, Beave, if you always did what your Dad told you to do, you would never have any fun"—did

BGA Headmaster Paul Reddick is pictured in the 1964 annual with the humorous caption: "I usta be a sailor myself."

not apply when you were on the receiving end of a violent head thrashing, made to crouch on your knees while your "cotton was picked," or were required to be at Goat's Rock-a-Rosa for a Saturday of fun. You can form your own opinion as to all of that, but for me, I am thankful we had it.

I matriculated at a school where I learned that poor behavior had a tangible consequence, one that usually terminated with an unpleasant result. To play off the words of our French professor Ralph Naylor, "Everybody has to be somewhere," I continually give thanks to my parents for making that "somewhere" a small boy's school in Franklin, Tenn., called Battle Ground Academy. Besides, serving off demerits by shining door knobs for the Stewart household on a fall Friday afternoon in 1963 wasn't so bad after all.

CHAPTER 14

Basketball Days

BACK BEFORE the interstate systems criss-crossed our country and people went for afternoon drives and road trips on two-lane highways, those meandering blacktops took us through the American countryside and through numerous small towns. Often, in the back of homes, if you looked closely, there would be a basketball goal, usually without a net, attached to the back of an old barn, garage door, on a tall plank at the end of a dirt driveway, or even in an open field. I always seemed to spot them.

A large open field across from our backyard, owned by the Herbert family, had one of those wooden goals stuck out in the middle of their property with grass and dirt as the playing surface, similar to what you would see on road trips back in the 1940s and '50s. It was eventually moved to our badminton court, built by my dad with help from Johnny Herbert (see "A Childhood Home" in the the book "When I Was a Kid"). I watched big kids play on the court, eventually becoming strong enough to

In 1953, the author (left) plays on the basketball court behind his childhood home, which featured a lowered goal for kids. Dribbling with him are Rhea and David Sumpter.

thrust the ball into a small goal built by my father just for me and other little kids who lived in the neighborhood. I learned to love the game, eventually advancing to the "big goal" and spending countless hours on our court over the years.

In March 1958, several of us seventh- and eighth-graders went to Vandy's Memorial Gym to watch the high-school state championships. I remember that little Lenoir City won it all…but what sticks out was a rather embarrassing spill by a patron just behind where we were sitting, which was up against the rail in Section F.

A large walkway just behind us provided a buffer zone before Section FF rose up with additional seating. A minute or so prior to the game, a young child had thrown up his lunch in the middle of that walkway, and it had yet to be cleaned up. With everyone seated, and the contest now in the early stages, a patron came around the corner in a semi-run, all decked out in his suit with his coat unbuttoned. As he began to slow down, his feet came in contact with the remnants of the youngster's noontime meal. Both feet flew out from under him, causing a quick reaction by his right hand in an effort to brace the fall. It worked. Unfortunately, his hand, the tail of his coat and cuffs of his pants, all hit the slimy mess at the same time. Because this occurred between two sections of seating, most everyone witnessed the event. He quickly righted himself, surveyed his stained suit, picked up his soiled glasses and tried to adjust his disheveled hair. Thoroughly disgusted, he slowly turned around and walked back to the entrance from which he came. Adults muffled their gasps, but us kids…not so. We all giggled loudly, adding to his humiliation. To this day, that event is still clear as a bell. I hope the patron put it out of his mind. I haven't.

As a player for Battle Ground Academy in Franklin, until graduating in 1965, I was afforded the opportunity to play, not only against city kids in Nashville, but also against small-town boys in a number of gymnasiums across southern Middle Tennessee. As a sophomore, I once attempted to defend Jimmy "Monk" Montgomery in the Middle Tennessee Invitational Tour-nament (MTIT) at Franklin High School in 1962. Monk was a 6-foot-5-inch legend from the small school of Kittrell, in the Murfreesboro area. On this occasion, he dribbled down the sideline, faded away some 20 feet from the hoop, and released his shot while falling into the bleachers. By the time the ball swished through the net, he was watching it from the first row. It was just two of over 4,000 points he chalked up in his career.

My efforts went unnoticed.

A few months later, in February 1963, Willie Brown of Father Ryan, who was the first black player to break the color barrier for Nashville sports, came to play at our gym in Franklin. It was a huge event. He was a step above the players we had been used to playing against. A month later, our squad returned to Memorial Gym in the 1963 TSSAA State Tourney and eked out a 69-67 win over Nashville's best team, the Donelson Dons. "The rip roaring capacity crowd of 7,000 rocked the rafters," wrote Raymond Johnson in The Nashville Tennessean. Our fans rushed the court at the final horn. It was a big deal for our little school.

West High School's gym, with walls only a few feet behind the goals, is pictured during a 1960 game.

Willie, Monk, and the Dons will be vividly remembered for a long time.

Our George I. Briggs gym at BGA was not new, having been constructed in 1948, and was nothing special. Seating was in the hundreds, not thousands. It was small and had those moon-shaped goals along the sidelines, which became part of the game strategy at times. They were never retracted during games. Aside from that, there were just 10 or so rows of metal bleachers on each side. Our glass backboards were offset maybe 10 feet from the wall. It did get loud in there. The gym was located at the end of the football field, and sported six huge windows, underneath which was a below-ground, bricked, enclosed space. Those windows looked out over the track, gridiron

Central High School's gym (top), known as "the pit" by some, is pictured in 1961 as cheerleaders perform a halftime show. Battle Ground Academy's George I. Briggs Gymnasium (bottom) is the uppermost building, pictured in 1962.

and beyond to the dining hall, classrooms and dormitories.

In the fall of 1963, they provided some near tragic happenings when several of us decided to play some pickup ball. When we arrived, it was discovered that the facility was locked, so we went down underneath where the locker room entrance was, but that was boarded up as well. Shaking all doors, exits and stopping just short of smashing glass, it came to our attention that the last window on the southeast end was slightly ajar. The only problem was that it was 20 feet up. Kids can be resourceful at times, especially when something is desired and there is a little bit of questionable behavior involved.

Rummaging around the facility, we came across a long wooden ladder, walked it around to the base of the large window, and hoisted it up to the opening. While my comrades stabilized it, I climbed up and proceeded to pry open the window just enough so we could squeeze through. It was a decent drop to the floor, but bleachers were there, so it was manageable. Steadying the ladder was no problem, that is until the last person had to climb up. We all ascended safely and managed to wriggle through the opening. Paul was last. Watching the ladder tips from the inside of the gym, we noticed it wobbling as young Paul's foot scaled each rung. With no one to hold it in place, he was on his own. After what seemed like an eternity, his hand appeared inside the window. We thought, "Great, all have made it in." Not to be, for as his other hand made a cameo appearance, the ladder gave way, sliding down the brick exterior of our gymnasium with a scraping, crashing sound only to be outdone by the screams of a 15-year-old free-falling some 20 feet into the bottom of the enclosed space beneath the window. We all just looked at each other, hoped Paul was still alive, divided up teams and began to play ball. Paul eventually righted the ladder and made his second attempt a success. Noticeably hobbling on two sprained ankles, his competitiveness was not diminished.

We had a great time that day, but I still wonder why I didn't push open the gym door and let everyone in after I scaled the wall. I guess the thrill of watching everyone enter through the window was exciting. Sorry, Paul.

Our team played legendary coach and neighbor Joe Shapiro's West High Blue Jays every year, in both home and away games. The old gym at West was a different animal, seemingly not made for safety. The benches were just off the court boundary, while the goals were hung no more than three feet from the brick wall that encompassed the court. A hard foul into that and your team best have plenty of substitutes. Fans sat all around looking down on the action. It was unique, for sure. I was fortunate to have played there from 1962 to 1964, about the last year it was used.

By the state fairgrounds, the Central High School gym was somewhat similar. The atmosphere in that facility was reminiscent of a Lions-versus-Christian thing. The only folks allowed on the floor were the combatants, officials, cheerleaders and coaches. It was a special place we called "the pit." Those Tornadoes were tough to beat in there. When we played Hume-Fogg High, there was an elevated floor, with a stage at one end, while the spectators watched the action from the side. Here, if one was to go flying to the sideline uncontrollably, you could end up in the gallery. You had to be careful. On Elliston Place, Father Ryan had a gym floor that was laid on top of concrete. After the third quarter, your legs would start to give out. It was a distinct home-court advantage.

Playing in a different district than Nashville gave me a look at what basketball was like in country towns. In Franklin, those tall, colorful cardboard game schedules were displayed in barber shops and local drug stores to promote the local team. These were commonplace. Those country gyms ranged from a couple of rows of seating to three levels, often with the lower one just inches from the playing surface. A high-school game in those communities was a big event. For weekend games, folks would gather early in the afternoon, often bringing in enough food for the entire family. That was allowed in some places. It was a regular town happening as the small communities got behind their local teams, often with excessive vigor, in particular when our small private school came calling.

In one of those heated games at Lawrenceburg High in January 1964, an unruly local, wearing some kind of bizarre-looking chef's hat, kept shouting unflattering remarks in my direction as I would bring the ball up the court. I was having a decent game that night, which accentuated the chiding. I often chewed bubble gum while playing, and on this evening it came in handy. Dribbling up court in the fourth quarter, I finally decided enough was enough. As the "Chef" stood up, bellowing whatever with that stupid hat, my last bubble was blown, and the juicy tidbit was extracted and fired up in the crowd in his direction. He saw it coming and ducked just as it struck his prized headgear. Of course, others chimed in after that, but I got a good laugh out of it, made my point, and tallied 28 points. It was too bad we lost the game 61-49.

This game schedule poster features the Battle Ground Academy Wildcats, for which the author played. Typical for the time, the cardboard posters were hung in store front windows.

That same night, at the wheel of my parents' early 1960s Chevy wagon enroute back to Franklin with four other players, a race ensued on the Spring Hill Highway (Highway 31) with fellow teammate John Paine, who was trying to keep pace in his car. There were a couple of long straight-a-ways between Columbia and Spring Hill, affording opportunities for us to push the limits. With no fear of death or for the safety of others, we buried the speedometer; 110 mph was as far as it would go. Paine was slowly disappearing in the distance as we crested a hill just before the city limits, when a state trooper's flashing lights appeared. I immediately backed off the accelerator, but it was too late. I was waived over by a Sergeant McCord. Several seconds later, he did the same thing to John. Now both of us were off to the side of the road as the rest of the team drove by. Paine wore contacts and the blowing dust caused his eyes to tear up and his hand to rub his face. Those in the following vehicles thought he was being beaten. Not to be, at least by the officer, but probably at home later.

Original caption from the Dec. 30, 1964, Nashville Tennessean: "Franklin, Tenn.—Airborne Tommy Henderson of Battle Ground Academy appears unhappy after Lipscomb's Eddie Green rushed by and smacked the ball into the air during the Middle Tennessee Invitational semifinal game." The author disputes the Tennessean's description of the encounter. (Nashville Public Library, Nashville Room, photo by Turner Hutchinson)

I was told by the trooper: "If I put you down for the speed you were actually going, you would lose your license. You were off the radar."

After determining we were part of the BGA basketball team, he said: "How about that, I arrested your headmaster for speeding earlier in the evening."

He put both Paine and me down for 70 in a 55-mph zone. Driving back to court in Lawrence County was no fun, as our parents had to go with us. When the judge called us in he said: "Boys, put your feet up on my desk." This took us by surprise, but we complied. He then came with: "You boys both are down

The unusual basketball uniforms of the Madison High School Rams were red with black and white polka dots. Picture is the 1965 team (left to right): front row: Larry Kirk, Jimmy Howard, Alex Beavers, Tommy Squires and Don Traylor; back row: Sammy Wolfe, Steve Moore, Ronnie Deweese, John Calloway, Steve Hunt and Larry Smith. (Metro Archives)

for 70 mph. That seems kind of strange since you, son, have a much bigger foot." He was pointing at John, who was 6 feet 2 inches, while I was 5 feet 10 inches. We did not say a word. The verdict was a stiff fine followed by, "If, in the future, you kids ever appear in my courtroom, you will never drive again in this county." Yes, sir.

I made my point in the Lawrenceburg game with that "Chef," but did not fare too well in other events. A few months later, when playing ball in a hay barn on my uncle's farm, dorm student Andy Mitchell said he had only five minutes to get back to school or miss curfew. About five miles away out on Columbia Pike, I said there is no way to make it unless I floor it. I said: "Will you pay the fine if I get a ticket?" Andy agreed. I got a ticket—by none other than officer McCord. After pulling me over, he looked into the car and said: "You again, Tom?" I was cited for driving barefooted and speeding, and I had to attend a driving class. Andy did NOT remain true to his word. Fortunately, I was not in Lawrence County.

In December 1964, The Nashville Tennessean, covering the MTIT in Franklin, displayed a photo of a Lipscomb player and myself with an incorrect caption, stating the Lipscomb player had "smacked the ball into the air." Smacked was right, but it was my arm he hammered. I am portrayed as "unhappy," which was about all that was correct. It was an unflattering photo anyway. There was nothing I could do about that mistake and no one at whom to lash out.

The other involved a return trip by Lawrenceburg in January 1965 to our gym, where legendary referee Burl Crowell whistled me for a technical foul after I jumped up and complained after a blocking call failed to go my way. Making the scene look worse than it was, my teammates immediately restrained me, as if I was going to attack the official. When our coach, Billy Smith, asked what I had done, Crowell stated, "He cussed me, coach." It was a complete fabrication. No vulgarities involved. Adding insult to injury, our headmaster, Paul Reddick, told coach Smith after the game to "keep me under control." I am glad I had no bubble gum that night.

From the '50s through the '60s, uniforms were both plain and unique. Coach Bill Brimm of Madison High wanted a different look for his Ram team, to attract attention and spice up things. That he did. Out they came with polka-dot gear in the 1960s. He once said, "People would pack the gymnasium just to see those polka dots." Some coaches complained they were a distraction, which was not disputed. On top of that, his teams were good. Those uniforms got national attention in a March 14, 1960, Sports Illustrated issue.

Our team had a complete wardrobe. We always came on the floor dressed out in dark blue, button-up wool warm-ups, underneath which was a "shooting" jersey that zipped, emblazoned with the school logo. Our blue-and-gold game attire was complete with short, embroidered game pants, with belt, 3-D-type numbers, and blue-and-gold socks up to the knee. If nothing else, we looked like we could play.

These few round-ball musings can take the mind in many different directions, most of which bring a smile to my face. I can also say they conjure up memories of poor judgment, questionable reporting and officiating, and at times unsportsmanlike antics. I do have regrets. For one, I am sorry I never apologized to official Burl Crowell—for NOT cussing him, therefore justifying the technical foul I was given. I sure wish that Lawrenceburg fan in the silly chef's hat would not have ducked, and that Andy would have paid my fine. Oh well, I guess I am just an "unhappy" basketball player. More bubble gum, please.

CHAPTER 15

1974

THE YEAR 1974 began another life phase for me. We had a three-inch snowfall on Jan. 10, which is always noteworthy, but that calendar year was also the first full one where I entered "the real world." Fulfilling my military obligations and graduating college finally meant it was time to enter the workforce on a permanent basis. Still in our 20s, my wife and I had come back to Nashville in 1973 and moved into a sprawling apartment complex at 6565 Premier Drive, off of Annex Avenue in West Nashville. We did not last long there.

Since 1966, when I last had an official residence in town, our city had changed. Not for the better, as far as I was concerned. Drug use had escalated in our culture more than ever, and the permissiveness of the late 1960s was on full display. Banging on our apartment door late one Saturday night, a hallucinating individual demanded entrance; he said he was cold. I politely told him, in no uncertain terms, to leave. It was to no avail, as he continued to hammer away.

The author's father, Tom Henderson Jr., stands in his front yard after a 3-inch snow in January 1974.

With my wife and 2-year old inside, I quickly phoned our local police, loaded my 410 shotgun, and said I would make him colder than he already was if he continued. The local authorities showed up 30 minutes later, well after the out-of-control fellow had heeded my demand. It was fortunate for him.

Within the next month or so we had someone burst in the front door while I was sitting on the couch. My dog Bogey aggressively escorted him out. I followed the sprinting intruder as he disappeared over the hill behind our apartment. Later, as my wife was alone in the complex's laundry room for over 30 minutes waiting on clothes to dry, an individual appeared from a closet door and nonchalantly walked out. That finished us. We began looking for a house the next week.

An AP Wirephoto released at the time of the murder, captioned: "SLAIN OPRY STAR— Grand Ole Opry and Hee Haw star Stringbean, whose name was really David Akeman, shows off the costume and down-home country humor that made him famous with country music fans around the world." (Nashville Public Library, The Nashville Room)

Thanks to a Veterans Administration loan, we settled in during the month of March at our new place just across Harding Road from the famous eatery and lodging destination, the Belle Meade Motel. One of the selling points of our new home was the "fabulous" shag carpets, a big thing during those times. A small child could disappear in the middle of the floor in that stuff. At the motel we often enjoyed some fine catfish, fried chicken, steak and biscuits and that crumbly blue-cheese dressing. Fresh turnip greens and even frog legs could be ordered. It was classic Southern food and a place where many had eaten a decade or two earlier. The motel itself was a shocker to some out-of-town friends after we suggested they stay there one evening. I was later told when I asked about the accommodations: "I opened the front door and fell across the bed." It was more of a "one night stand" type place.

Original caption from the April 4, 1974, Nashville Banner: "There's little remaining of this home on Pettus Road that stood in the path of a twister late Wednesday. Furnishings in the home were thrown more than 100 feet from the structure." (Nashville Public Library, Nashville Room, photo by Owen Cartwright)

That same month, the television show "Hee Haw" aired Stringbean Ackerman's last performance (the scarecrow in the cornfield). He had been murdered in 1973. Convictions were handed down in November. President Nixon spoke at the dedication of the new Opry House on the grounds of Opryland U.S.A. amusement park, and a little-known rock group, Lynyrd Skynyrd, performed at Muther's Music Emporium on Hermitage Avenue before a scant crowd of 100 or so. They, along with Blue Oyster Cult, later entertained at the Tennessee State Fair. I recall fiddling-great Charlie Daniels starting his Volunteer Jam at the War Memorial Building as well. We were not in attendance at any of those events but did eventually watch Nixon give his final salute when leaving office amid the Watergate scandal.

April came, and our city was besieged by a tornado outbreak. In 1973, the roof of our apartment had been blown off by one, so we were on the lookout. It happened on April 3 and 4. We put pillows on our heads, got in the bathtub and hoped for the best. Bogey shook like he had been in an ice bath, cowering in the bathroom closet. We avoided the devastation, but those folks southeast of town had a rough time. The Battle of Nashville monument (on Franklin Pike at the time) had the obelisk and angel destroyed as well. Damage was extensive. It became one of the largest tornado outbreaks ever in our city and in the country. The next week we returned to normalcy, and we watched Hank Aaron break Babe Ruth's home-run record. A whirlwind of opinions surrounded that event. Later in the year, another baseball favorite, Dizzy Dean, passed away.

Cooper and Martin grocers' "Let's Go to the Races" was still being aired by WNGE Channel 2 television, one of only four channels we could get back then, along with WSM, WLAC and WDCN Channel 8. Those local stations brought us "The Andy Griffith Show," numerous soap operas, "Mike Douglas," "M*A*S*H," "Good Times," "Gomer Pyle" and "Happy Days." The cornball comedy "Green Acres," "The Newlywed Game" and "Password" were all part of regular programming.

In the summer, Paul McCartney and his Wings band recorded at the Sound Shop studios, staying at Curly (Junior) Putman's farm in Wilson County, riding dirt bikes while there. Unfortunately, we were not invited out to the farm. Instead, we spent time in Monteagle at the Rock n' Rest cabin where my son, Todd, popped his first bubble-gum bubble that my wife blew. He was later read Mother Goose nursery rhymes by my mama. You can't beat that.

In October, another music superstar of that time, Alice Cooper, teed it up at the new Harpeth Hills Golf Course in the Music City Pro-Celebrity

Original headline and caption from the July 16, 1974, Nashville Banner: "With A Touch Of Reality— Southbound motorists on I-65 slowed down a bit Monday as they viewed this 'wreck' at the Shelby Street exit. However, it was all part of a filming sequence in the movie Nashville being filmed here. From a distance, though, it was difficult to believe the bus, cars and police vehicles were just part of a celluloid world." (Nashville Public Library, Nashville Room, photo by Don Foster)

Golf Tournament. I hope no snakes were in his bag. If golf did not appeal to you, then there was the Tri-State Baseball league, still a big hit at Centennial Park. One game featured Haury and Smith against Tennessee Pride Eggs, whose players were affectionately called the Eggmen. It was fun to watch.

During July and August, the movie "Nashville" was filmed all over town, including a faked traffic accident on I-65 at Shelby Street. The Parthenon provided a set, too, using mostly locals as extras who just happened to be watching at the time. The film was released in 1975. Speaking of movies, at the 100 Oaks Martin Theater, "Airport '75" hit the screen. The Tennessee Theatre featured Burt Reynolds, who was dating Nashville's Dinah Shore, in "The Longest Yard," and down at the Belle Meade Theater, "The Sting" had an extended stay. Over in Hillsboro Village, the Belcourt used both screens; on one was "Hot Times" with the teaser "High School Daze," while Belcourt 2 projected "Gather Moss" with the Rolling Stones. That had to be a classic. I am afraid we missed both of those jewels. The frightening "Exorcist" and the irreverent "Blazing Saddles" were released and made their stops in town as well.

The Oscars that year saw Master of Ceremonies David Niven at the

Original headline and caption from the April 10, 1974, Tennessean: "Only the Bold Need Apply—Lady Godivas who would like a free alignment have a golden opportunity, according to this sign at Tom Polk Tire Co., 125 12th Ave., S." (Nashville Tennessean, photo by Kit Luca)

podium when a buck-naked lad raced past him and exited stage left. The show had just been "streaked," a fad going on at that time, mainly among college kids. Niven's response: "Isn't it fascinating that the only laugh that man will ever get is for stripping and showing his shortcomings." Nashville's own Ray Stevens capitalized, hitting the top spot in music with his recording of "The Streak" ("don't look Ethel...too late, she had already been incensed"). Joining the nude theme, the Nashville Banner ran a story on a UCLA student running for governor on the Peace and Freedom ticket. She was photographed, naked, passing out literature protesting the ban on nudity. Evidently the Oscars' streaker was a member of that party, too.

This advertisement for Playhouse Cinema appeared in the Nov. 18, 1974, Nashville Banner. *(Tennessee State Library and Archives)*

"Sweet Home Alabama" (Lynyrd Skynyrd), "Ramblin Man" (Allman Brothers) and "Come and Get Your Love" (Native-American group Redbone), rose in the charts but couldn't quite top Stevens' novelty record. On a sad note musically, Mama Cass of the Mamas and Papas group died. The rumor was she choked on a ham sandwich.

July 19 brought James Brown to the Municipal Auditorium for only $5.50 a ticket (in advance). A $1,000 award was given away to the best-dressed man and lady. I am told there were some fine threads on display that evening...just not mine. I had already seen James and the Famous Flames at a blistering outdoor venue in 1968, in Vietnam.

If you had "discriminating" tastes, Nashville covered that as well. The Midtown Cinema at 613 Church Street was a popular destination for the consenting adult. Lower Broad became a hot spot for this stuff, particularly after the Grand Ole Opry moved to Opryland. There was the Consenting Adult

Original caption from the Nov. 18, 1974, Nashville Banner: "The Rev. Mel Perry, center, led a demonstration Sunday in front of the WSM-TV studios on Knob Hill Road protesting the NBC airing of the film The Godfather. Also objecting to the film's showing was the Rev. Bobby Flatt, left, and the Rev. Howard Hall." (Nashville Public Library, Nashville Room, photo by Don Foster)

Theater at 116 Sixth Ave. S., the Playhouse Cinema at 423 Broadway, and the All New Adult Theater at Seventh and Commerce. The Avant-Garde Film Club at 108 Third Ave. N. let "ladies" in free, if escorted. I can think of no better place to take a date. The Fourth Avenue Book Mart featured 25-cent mini movies—buy one get four free. That's a bargain even grandma would like.

Lower Broad was not the hangout spot for us. The Reverend Mel Perry frequently protested around these spots, but on Nov. 18 he and 60 others descended on the WSM-TV studios to voice their opposition to Channel 4 showing the two-part series, "The Godfather." It all caused quite a disturbance but had no effect on programming.

Big cars still ruled, even though there was a fuel crisis going on. Long lines became the norm at the pumps. Red Ace gas stations gave away 500 Top Value stamps for a fill-up to attract customers. Thankfully our Volkswagen wagon was fuel-efficient, and gas was around 55 cents a gallon. To try to limit fuel consumption, President Nixon signed the National Speed Limit Law, forcing everyone to drive no more than 55 miles per hour. Sorry to say this, but I became a law breaker.

I am not sure what they did about conserving airline fuel, but air traffic continued at a steady level. Just as my father had taken me to the old Berry Field to watch the planes take off and land (see "A Trip to the Airport" in the book "Yesterdays"), I did the same with my son, and took Dad with us, too. The terminal had changed, but security was still lax. You could go out into the grassy area on a hill by the old Avco plant on Briley Parkway, spread a blanket down, and watch the action. The tarmac wasn't far off.

The magic of flight continued as the model airplane field in Edwin Warner Park captured our fancy. We often went there, mingling with the pilots and planes. It was exciting for our young son. To add to the fun, just across the street, there was a colorful merry-go-round and see-saw. We took advantage of those, too, as most were being phased out, unfortunately.

October and November had the usual sales, political news and headliner sporting events in our papers. None was much bigger than the "Rumble in the Jungle" heavyweight boxing match in Zaire, featuring champ George Foreman against Muhammad Ali (Cassius Clay). Just about everyone watched or heard about that one. Not a sporting event, but a race nonetheless, was Ray Blanton's winning the governor's job after earlier defeating

In 1974, the author and his son, Todd, visited a field next to Avco at Berry Field airport to watch planes take off and land (left) and went to Edwin Warner Park for the merry-go-round (right).

This advertisement for B and W Cafeteria appeared in the Nov. 18, 1974, Nashville Banner. (Tennessee State Library and Archives)

bank magnate Jake Butcher in the Democratic primary election. Butcher was operating United American Bank, formerly Hamilton Bank, here in town and elsewhere. Sad to say but both of those character's careers ended up in disasters.

Holiday sales began in earnest with the year's big novelty item, the Magic 8 Ball. Roll it over and it would predict your future. If you didn't like what it said, roll it over again. Our future always looked good. We got our seasonal gift baskets at the Sunshine Shop at 1912 Church St. That same gift basket served well for births and deaths. Super 8 movie cameras were selling from $68 to $139, depending on where you went. We shot a lot of family film with one of those. When filming inside, you had to hold a highly-illuminated spotlight in one hand while shooting with the other. Many movies show family members covering their eyes for protection.

Restaurants and grocers offered up their best later in the year. Cooper and Martin, for Thanksgiving, sold oysters at $1.99 for a 12 oz. can, and turkeys went from 39 cents to 59 cents a pound. They accepted those highly-prized Quality Stamps, too. As far as dining out, we often went to Spats at 1601 21st Ave. S. in Hillsboro Village. They touted the "World's Greatest Bar-B-Que Ribs," and the Budweiser on tap was only 45 cents. College kids liked that; so did I. Yannies in Green Hills had a Saturday-night special that included a 10 oz. ribeye for $2.69. On Sunday they laid out a buffet for $1.95. Shoney's feature was the Fisherman's Platter for $1.99, while on Monday it was all the spaghetti you could eat for $1.55 (with tossed salad). Ireland's on 21st, famous for their steak and biscuits, advertised a filet mignon dinner for $2.50. That was some deal. The Smuggler's Inn on Murfreesboro Road rivaled it with their "Steak for Two," including baked potato, soup and salad, for $5.25. For my money nothing could quite beat the B and W Cafeteria. They had lunch for a whopping 77 cents and a dinner for $1.23, consisting of spaghetti and meatballs, bread and sweet slaw... yum, yum. They also advertised "A Complete Holiday Turkey Package," already fixed for the entire family, for the low price of only $15.95. Kuhn's Variety Store, not known for food, gave away one 10- to 12-pound turkey every hour just to get customers. Nothing could beat the offer from Dairy Queen, however. They had a "scrumpdillyishus" chili dog for 49 cents, boasting it was "almost a foot long."

The author's first Christmas tree in his new family's home (notice the deep shag carpet)

Thanksgiving came and went without incident, other than a one-and-a-half-inch rain that flooded Richland Creek the week before.

Finally, Christmas arrived. We visited all the relatives, just as we did on Thanksgiving, trekking from one home to the next, just enjoying the season. I put up a Christmas tree in our own house for the first time and, with the help of my wife, trimmed it just like we both had done growing up. Nothing elaborate—just a tree. It was quite a spectacle resting on the shag carpet. Charlie Brown would have been proud.

On New Year's Eve we usually went partying, prevailing on my parents to babysit while we acted like kids. That year, however, we decided to stay and celebrate with my folks on Cantrell Avenue. Mother provided the non-alcoholic party favors, complete with the festive, tacky hats and the flute-like

Above is the author's first Christmas tree in his new family's home (notice the deep shag carpet). Below, the Henderson family celebrates New Year's Eve 1974 in the playroom at 700 Cantrell Ave. Front row (left to right): Carolyn Henderson (wife) and Lynn White (sister). On couch: Vance Wheeler (nephew), Amy Wheeler (niece), Genevieve Selph (mother-in-law) and Kathy Wheeler (niece). Back row: Hal Selph (brother-in-law), Bay Henderson (mother), the author, and Doug White (brother-in-law).

toys we blew to ring in the new year. It was a low-key affair, just what we needed.

The year 1974 sure started out much different than it ended. Compared to a drug addict banging on the door, a would-be felon making an unannounced entrance into our apartment, a pervert lurking in the shadows in a laundry room, tornados ripping through neighborhoods, and streakers appearing from nowhere, low-key was a good thing. For a couple of kids starting out in their first home, with a youngster in tow, it turned out to be a pretty good year. I kind of liked 1974.

CHAPTER 16

Blowing Smoke

Smoke, smoke, smoke that cigarette
Puff, Puff, Puff
And if you smoke yourself to death,
Tell St. Peter at the Golden Gate
That you hates to make him wait
You've gotta have another cigarette
—Tex Williams, "Smoke, Smoke, Smoke
(That Cigarette)" (1947)

IT WASN'T that bad. It was just a cool thing to do...I guess. Once in the military, it became a little more than that. In WWI and WWII, Camels were part of the soldier's rations. That had ended by the time I came along. At about age 15, I had my first tobacco inhale, when a friend pulled out a pack of cigarettes and passed out a couple. This was Big Time, not like when we used to light up pieces of grapevine with the occasional worm inside, thinking we were hot stuff. This was all about being "with it." It was a grown-up, independent thing. I had inhaled one time before, at age 12, resulting in an up-chucking of Spaghetti-Os. Not a pleasant sight.

Our local papers ran half-page advertisements on the glories of smoking, showing everyone from your favorite actor, sports hero, and television star, to doctors and dentists, all touting the wonders of the weed. This had to be good stuff. "Rebel Without A Cause" star James Dean was super cool, rolling up a pack of Marlboros in his shirt sleeve and donning a leather jacket. In 1958, Castner-Knott department store ran an ad for a windbreaker, depicting a model holding a cigarette. We all watched a rugged, good-looking,

Winston cigarettes were a sponsor of "The Flintstones," an animated TV program that originally aired in prime-time from 1960 to 1966. (YouTube)

wrinkle-free individual, called the Marlboro Man, give the vibe that it was manly to smoke, and in 1960 we watched the Flintstones light each other a Winston in a TV commercial. How bad could smoking be? There was a subtle hint in 1965 that something was not good when the Surgeon General put warnings on cigarette packages, but before that, and in 1963 when smoking peaked, us kids had no fear.

> *A-checking out the halls,*
>   *makin' sure the coast is clear*
> *Lookin' in the stalls,*
>   *no there ain't nobody here.*
> *Oh, my buddy Fang, and me and Paul*
>   *to get caught would surely be the death of us all,*
> *Smokin' in the boys room,*
> *Now teacher don't you fill me*
>   *up with your rules,*
> *But everybody knows that smokin'*
>   *ain't allowed in school*
> —Brownsville Station, "Smokin' in the Boys Room," (1973)

At Woodmont Elementary, I stayed clear of the boys bathroom. Foul doings by the eighth graders went on in there. One of the only times I entered, I was smacked in the face by what looked to be a massive cloud bank, emitting an odor reminiscent of a road-kill armadillo and a neighbor burning wet leaves. I never graced that facility again. At my high school, Battle Ground Academy in Franklin, there was a small four-by-four tin "smoke shack," built sometime before 1955 and situated at the rear of the dining hall, halfway hidden by some bushes, for use by boarders to keep those cloud banks out of the restrooms. Dorm students apparently had a nicotine habit that proved too much for the proctors to monitor. A note from a parent was all that was required to enter. This was clearly an effort to identify the smokers and keep their butts in one area, and, believe me, there were a lot of butts in that shack, even up until the time I graduated in 1965.

According to one former BGA student, Dick Jewell, Jim Eddie's Pool Hall on Main Street, next door to the theater and the fire hall, required no parental consent to smoke. To that I can testify. Several BGA boys were suspended from the football team, having been caught in there puffing away on some Marlboros during an eight-ball game. Dick recalls the smoke was at

Jim Eddie's Pool Hall (to the left of Franklin Theatre in this circa 1940 photo) allowed youths to smoke on its premises. However, school authorities at nearby Battle Ground Academy did not. (Rick Warwick)

times so thick it was hard to see the cue ball. You didn't have to buy cigarettes at all if you went to the picture show, because everyone watching the movie got the fumes for free.

In Nashville, at West High School in 1959, Morgan Harrub, Bill Killingsworth and others decided to take a few drags near a back door before first period. There was no better way to start off the day than to suck away on a Lucky Strike or puff on a cigar. They thought they were tough, until the door abruptly opened and out came Coach Kennedy. The cigs made a rapid disappearance, but the cigar, smoked by Killingsworth, was quickly shoved in his Levi jeans back pocket.

"Mr. Kennedy talked to us for several minutes, then went back inside," Morgan said. "Bill's pants were smoldering, and he was slapping his butt trying to put the sparks out. The rest of us were cracking up."

Let us hope Bill's backside fared better than the Levis. That same year in January, when Fidel Castro ran Batista out of Cuba, our country was initially unaware he was a communist.

"We West High boys would wear black tee shirts and chant 'Give em' hell Fidel,'" Morgan said. "It was considered 'cool' to smoke Lucky Strikes

These newsies in St. Louis, Mo., were photographed smoking in 1910. (Library of Congress)

and keep a pack rolled up in the sleeve of our black tee shirt. When the truth came out [about Fidel], we quit doing that. I gave that black shirt to my girlfriend, who slept in it every night. We've been married 53 years."

Let's hope that pack of Luckies left about the time Batista did, or we have a scoop on our hands.

Apparently Coach Kennedy was the smoking sergeant-at-arms for several years, because in 1964, Doug Stephenson and pals were apprehended under a concealed area by a road that

James Dean holds a cigarette in this publicity still for the 1955 movie "Rebel Without a Cause." (Wikipedia)

bordered the school. Doug said there was a spot on Bowling Avenue that was below ground level, "where you could scoot down the bank, two to three feet, sit down and not be seen. We thought if we scrunched down, no one would see us. He [Kennedy] couldn't, but when you have seven to eight guys smoking, there is going to be a cloud."

No kidding, Doug.

"Kennedy caught several of us that day, and I think I got some licks, but I had plenty of those over the years," Doug said. "I never got caught for the really bad stuff."

I'm told that the fuse of a cherry bomb inside the end of a Lucky, lit it and placed in the cafeteria, under a warming tray of succotash, would explode in about five minutes, giving one time to escape. In my book, this would classify as "bad stuff." I am not positive this ever happened at West, but I am sure it did somewhere.

That same year, to try to get a handle on the smokers, Nancy James(Clark) said the administration allowed smoking only in the first floor bathroom, for

Basketball star Bob Cousy endorsed Kent cigarettes in this 1962 advertisement. (fairwarning.org)

a short period of time. "We thought we were so cool. It was rather short-lived due to the sloppy smokers." Too many butts in there, I guess. I assume that is when Doug and his pals headed for Bowling Avenue.

Hillsboro High had rules, too, and no smoking on school grounds was one of them. Al Battle and his brother had grown up smoking grapevine and rolled-up brown paper bags, just to emulate his folks, who were chronic smokers. Those makeshift "fags," as we used to call them, gave off a foul taste and eventually led to a pilfering of his parents' weeds. I can't say I blame him, because anything would be an improvement over that. At Hillsboro, he would often head to the boys bathroom, with other ne'er-do-wells, just to get a puff or two before the next class. Teachers periodically checked the restrooms during this time. Lookouts provided some warnings by stating the teacher's name very loud.

"It was not uncommon to hear a kid holler: 'Hello, Coach Coutras, Hello Mr. Hatcher, Hello Coach Nance,'" Al said. "All of those professors had classrooms near the restroom, and if they caught you with a cigarette in your hand or mouth, you were marched off to the principal's office and given a three-day suspension. Needless to say, many of us received these three-day passes, me included."

In the early 1970s, at Mt. Juliet High School, Assistant Principal Acuff monitored the designated smoking area with an air of fear.

"He was a strict disciplinarian of the old school variety," Susan Wilson said, which still included paddling. "He was very formidable looking and acting, and most everyone was terrified of him except the most 'renegade,' rebels-without-a-cause kids. Of course, this was the 1970s, and the smoking area was inhabited by the 'fringe group,' what were referred to as 'hippies' back then."

I sincerely doubt grapevine was the smoke of choice.

During my junior year at BGA, in 1963, cigarettes were not part of our basketball training regimen. Hall-of-fame basketball player at West under coach Joe Shapiro, Jimmy French, was our coach and would put up with none of that stuff, even though Boston Celtic star Bob Cousy endorsed Kent cigarettes. It was just before the 22nd District Tournament that "Ruby and the Romantics" unknowingly tested the waters. "Ruby" was a fellow squad member named Mike Ross. He, along with me and fellow point guard John Tompkins were deemed by Ross to be "the Romantics." I guess he liked that singing group and the hit song they put out, "Our Day Will Come." The opening lines went:

"Our day will come, and we'll have everything." It was a February afternoon, just north of school on the Columbia Pike, when we made our regular stop at the Dairy Queen to replenish after ball practice and decided to top it off with a Winston. Ross, a little-used substitute, and Tompkins, a starting guard, lit up, but I was otherwise occupied with eating and driving. With our windows slightly cracked, the smoke streamed out like a vapor trail during our ride home on Hillsboro Pike. We had no idea that Coach French happened to be on the same road, right behind

A model holds a cigarette in this detail from a 1958 Caster-Knott advertisement. (Tennessee State Library and Archives)

us. The next day we were called in to Coach's office and interrogated. Ross and Tompkins were seen smoking and had no choice but to admit wrongdoing. I, on the other hand, was somewhat shielded from French. When sternly questioned if I was smoking, I replied: "Not me, Coach. I was not. I had a DQ Freeze in one hand and an Ultimate Chili Dog and the steering column in the other." Judging from his paused, quizzical gaze, I could tell he doubted my innocence but had no choice but to let me go. As for Ross and Tompkins, they were kicked off the squad right before the district tourney.

Back then, no generic statements were given; everything was to the point: BGA players booted from the team for smoking. We had a poor tourney, even though I did make first team All District, but we lost in the semifinals, justly, I suppose. I was tainted for the rest of my high-school career in Coach French's eyes, for I am sure he thought I had lied. It could be said that Ruby and the Romantics' day had come and gone, just like the chili dog and the Freeze.

I gave a good effort to cut back smoking in 1967, going to the mild True Blue and True Green brand, but once in the military, a bona fide habit kicked in, and for almost three years it was two packs a day of anything, from the strongest-made Picayunes and Bull Durhams to Bugler, the kind you had to roll yourself. When I got out of the service in 1969, the warnings of lung cancer became more prominent. That is when I decided I was done with 'em. I threw the last pack out of the Ramada Inn window on James Robertson Parkway in downtown Nashville, where my wife and I spent my first night back from my tour in Vietnam. That was all she wrote, except for some middle-aged pipe-smoking to emulate my grandfather and uncle.

Tips breath-freshener was sometimes used by the author to cover up the fact that he had been smoking.

I never got caught smoking while growing up, and I thought my parents never knew. I know now that was not the case. I was required, after a night of gallivanting

The author gave up smoking at this downtown Nashville Ramada Inn in 1969, throwing his last pack out a window.

around town, to always come in and kiss my mother good night. It was mandatory, regardless of the hour. I really thought that my little bottle of Tips breath-freshener did the trick. Even when I would go upstairs to my room and open the window after lighting up, I felt that no one knew, other than my friends and my youngest sister, that is. She even took a few drags with me one time…forgive me, Sis. I know Mom never knew about that. What I am sure of is that being a devout Christian, she had pull with "the man upstairs," and always said an extra prayer on my behalf. I was fortunate that Mother had a lot of influence, because St. Peter is still waiting. I thank God for that.

Chapter 17

Beer, Wine & Whiskey

I went out last night
Finally knocked myself outta sight
I got full of that bad stuff
And almost started a fight
I'm now feeling just fine
I think I'll stop drinking whiskey,
     and going back to bad wine
Bad, bad whiskey
Bad, bad whiskey
     — Amos Milburn and his Aladdin Chickenshackers, "Bad, Bad Whiskey" (1950)

I HAVE TO say it wasn't bad whiskey that I taste tested at first—no, sir, it was the "Champagne of Bottled Beer," Miller High Life. I suppose after a few of those you were expected to experience the "High Life." I did, briefly. However, after three longnecks and sharing an extra large bag of Southern pork rinds, I fell to depths I had theretofore never known. This was not mentioned on the label.

It was in 1963 that three of us sophomores in high school persuaded upper-classman Granberry to buy us two six-packs at the local Jim Dandy Market. He was underage, as well, but was one of those kids who looked 21 when, in fact, he was only 17. He was rarely asked to present his identification. I can't thank him enough. About all I remember about that evening is a prolonged, epic stomach virus and one in which I was lucky to have retained my digestive system. I do recall waking up around 2 a.m. at a friend's home

The Jim Dandy market on Hillsboro Road is shown here circa 1965. The author's neighbor acquired beer via devious means from the one just like it on Kenner Avenue.

on the edge of his swimming pool, brought back to life by his family collie licking my cheeks. When I got back home, I struggled up the steps to my bedroom and slinked under the covers, closely followed by my mother. She sat on the end of my bed without saying a word…at first. I explained what I had done and vowed never, ever to have another drink in my entire life, and to give up barbeque pork rinds, after which I was quoted several passages from Proverbs, or one of those biblical chapters, about the evils of over-indulgence. A hearty dose of religion, time, and Phillips Milk of Magnesia made for a quick recovery.

About 8000 BC, the first Stone Age beer container was discovered, while wine first appeared in Egyptian pictographs about 4000 BC. It seems pyramid laborers got a daily ration of one-and-a-third gallons of beer for nourishment. It was believed to be a necessity of life, invented by the god Osiris. I can only imagine that after consuming that much beer, the next day a new work force must have been called into action.

As peer pressure increased, in my pre-college years, alcohol consumption came into play. Millions of us Baby Boomers took part in underage drinking. Not only were we trying to get away with something, but it was fun to get that buzzed feeling and to experience what it was like to be an "adult." It all

This Falstaff beer advertisement appeared in the March 5, 1964, Nashville Banner. Ads for alcoholic beverages usually ran in the sports section. (Tennessee Library and Archives)

combined for some inadvisable behavior.

Beer was the easiest to come by, because there were markets on just about every street corner. One was near the old Barbizon Apartment building, simply called Johnny's, a notorious distributor of alcohol to the underaged on 21st Avenue at Broadway. My friend Bruiser got some of his from Frank's Friendly on Charlotte Pike. Frank was friendly because they would watch for young teens.

"Just pull in the back," Bruiser said, "and there was always a man standing in the lot ready to get you a six-pack of Schlitz Malt Liquor or good old Oertels '92. We would tip him a dollar and lay a can on him."

In town there was a place called Tish Tosh on 11th Avenue North that specialized in Pabst Blue Ribbon quart bottles. There was a fellow down there who waited for kids to tip him, after which he would go inside and buy the stuff for you. Curbside service at its best.

At 911 Eighth Ave. N. was Al Jackson's market, which had dirt floors and a screened-in porch. There was a sign that said, "If you want the keg, you want the ice. If you don't want the ice, you don't want the keg." I guess Al had something going on with Noel Ice Company just down the road. There was an area in the back with tables outside where they would serve ice-cold drafts, but that was not for us kids. We could purchase beer by the case sometimes, and, as buddy Hal remembers, they had someone who would come to your car, take the old empty Schlitz bottles away, replace them with a new case and give you credit, all for a tip of 50 cents. Back then Schlitz bottles were refundable, so you didn't see them lying around. As the saying goes, "When you're out of Schlitz, you're out of beer." At Al's, if you put the cash on the counter, you would get the beer. Al also distributed that high-quality beverage, Colt 45 Malt Liquor, which came out in 1963. It was not top-of-the-line stuff. One kid put it this way: "This beer is not to be enjoyed, just drank quickly in preparation for a rowdy night. You gain a level of drunkenness but lose a great deal of dignity. I recall purchasing two of these at a very small local liquor store and having the clerk, an older Native man, ask if I wanted a paper bag so that I could, 'Sit on the curb with the rest of 'em.'"

Speaking of dignity, on a summer night in 1963, Moose, Alfred and I picked up a couple of quarts and a tall boy or two from Mrs. Mize's Southernaire Market at 1610 Church St. Identification at times was not necessary there. After a couple of hours of driving around in my two-door Fiat 500, Alfred, who was a novice at ingesting spirits, became increasingly nauseated, finally giving up the contents of his stomach somewhere near the Radnor rail yards. Unfortunately, several motorists passed by during his "illness." To see someone on all fours dry heaving,

Five Brothers bourbon was advertised in the Sept. 12, 1967, Nashville Banner. (Tennessee State Library and Archives)

This Yellowstone bourbon ad appeared in the March 3, 1964, Nashville Banner. (Tennessee State Library and Archives)

with movements that would make Rufus Thomas proud, had to be unsettling. It is still a mystery to me why some slowed down to witness such a spectacle. The engineer on the passing locomotive blowing his whistle might have attracted some attention. After several minutes of this, Moose and I assisted our friend into the back seat and motored off to fill up with gasoline at, I believe, a Gulf station on Hillsboro Pike, across from Crestmoor Road. Just as we pulled in, and ran over the hose that rings a bell notifying the clerk that someone needs fuel, Alfred leaned out of the window and finished what he had started in the rail yards. This time the remnants collected on the rear panel of the Fiat. I asked that attendant for a fill-up and requested a wiping off of what remained of my friend's evening meal. He took extreme exception to the request, which was understandable. The grizzled, uniformed man spouted a stream of obscenities followed by "you boys get the hell out of here." Yes, Colt 45 can cause a loss of dignity.

How could impressionable kids our age not give alcohol a try? Ads were abundant in magazines, on television and in our newspapers, particularly in the sports sections back in the 1960s. I guess the reasoning there was that if you lost an athletic contest, you could lessen the agony of defeat by getting loaded. I lost several athletic contests during my youth. Liquor advertisements in our paper ranged from Old Crow ("Is This the Greatest Name in Bourbon?"—we all knew that answer), Old Charter ("The Bourbon that didn't Watch the Clock"), Early Times, Old Barton and Heaven Hill (replacing the "e" with an "i" after the "v" would have been more appropriate). There was an ad for Five Brothers Bourbon and for Yellowstone, whose by-line was "That's Rite, No Bite!" Odd that it was placed just below a spot for Harvey's department store selling tear gas. That must have been meant for the folks that served Yellowstone to protect themselves from those who drank it.

As far as wine goes, kids went for the low end and a quick lift such as Ripple, Boones Farm, Mogan David, and MD 20/20 (what your vision was before you drank it). Above all, the top of the line, in what was known as "bum wine," was probably Cisco, followed closely by Night Train Express. (Tip: Always avoid cheap wine with the word "express" in it.) The undisputed dredge of the gutter wines was Thunderbird. Invented by Ernest and Julio Gallo in 1957 to corner the younger market, it instead became the top seller in ghettos. It sold for a whopping 60 cents a bottle. Check out their radio ad and slogan:

> *What's the word? Thunderbird*
> *How's it sold? Good and Cold*
> *What's the Jive? Bird's Alive*
> *What's the price? Thirty twice*

One critic's review after drinking some T-Bird says it all: "If your taste buds are shot, and you need to get trashed with a quickness, then T-Bird is the drink for you. Or, if you like to smell your hand after pumping gas, look no further than Thunderbird. We highly discourage drinking this ghastly mixture of unknown chemicals unless you really are a bum." The alcohol content was 17.5 percent, and that golden color of the liquid reportedly would turn your lips black. I shied away from T-Bird.

Beer ads ranged from the good stuff, Budweiser and Miller High Life, to Oertels '92, Falstaff (distributed locally by Johnny Beasley), Carling Black Label, Hamm's, Pabst Blue Ribbon, Lone Star, Country Club Malt Liquor, Malt Duck, Champale, and the aforementioned Colt-45 and Wiedemann. Wiedemann provided a number of us high school kids with weekend libation for several months, at no cost. How's that, you say? My neighbor was a part-time employee at the Kenner Avenue Jim Dandy Market back in the mid-1960s. Part of his responsibilities included restocking the beer, breaking down the boxes it came in, and carrying them outside to the big dumpster. After being pressured into borrowing a few six-packs during his Friday night shifts, he finally gave in. Noticing the manager would often turn up a pint of vodka to his lips as he sat in his office, my friend (name withheld due to statute of limitations) planned the caper: He would leave a box intact, place a case, or several six-packs of Wiedemann inside with the broken down boxes on top, and carry out the "trash" to the dumpster and deposit it. When his shift ended, he went back to the dumpster, retrieved the beer, and put it in the back of his mom's 1961 Ford Falcon, after which he would drop it off at classmate Jim West's back garage inside of the family's disabled 1953 Ford Sedan. Voila, free beer. Unfortunately, word traveled fast about his "enterprise" as inventory built up.

"Several times when I went to get the stash [at the dumpster], it was gone," he said. "Someone passed by [the market] while I was still working and absconded the beer. What dishonesty!"

A plan to get back at the thief for stealing from the thief was put in place.

"The next time, I went through my usual routine, but when I reached the dumpster, I set the beer on the ground, took off the broken boxes on top and peed all over a case of Wiedemann," he said. "I placed the beer in the dumpster, like always, and sure enough, someone had made off with it when I later checked. Hope they enjoyed the beer."

Eventually West's mother discovered the beer in the 1953 Ford and forced the boys to empty all the cases down the sink.

"God bless her, she never told my folks," he said. "It sure would give me joy to know who procured that case of beer."

We eventually moved from beer and wine to the "hard stuff." This required a different approach, as liquor stores were more stringent on checking your I.D., plus they were not located at most every intersection. Off we went to places that were not consistent with sustained life. We often drove toward the more depressed areas of town and usually tipped a local citizen to get us a fifth of something. On one of these excursions to Gleaves, at 1434 12th Ave. S., one such citizen was spotted. We were out of place in that area

Little Jimmy Dickens performs in front of an Oertels '92 beer logo at the Louisville Gardens in mid-1950s. (Ralph Mitchell)

because it was mostly a black section of town. Folks knew what a bunch of white kids with crew cuts trolling the area were looking for. Pulling alongside this individual in my friend's Corvair, the conversation went something like this: "Hey, man, how's it going? Can you get us a fifth of Jack in the Black? I got 20 bucks for you." His answer was, "Sure, just drive around the block and I will meet you here in few minutes."

After making several trips around and around and around, our courier did a disappearing act, along with the $20. About the fourth trip canvassing the area, we spotted him sitting on a legless sofa on a porch behind the store with about five other young men. None of them looked accommodating. I rolled down the window and said, "Did you get the stuff?" No reply. A little louder I yelled, "Hey, man, did you get the stuff?" Finally several of them rose to their feet and moved in our direction just as the one we gave our $20 to yelled, "Cool your heels, man." I tapped my friend's shoulder, who was driving, and said: "Let's get out of here." I hope the 20 bucks went for a down payment on a new Barcolounger.

Some of the things we did and places we went to get weekend alcohol would have led our folks to believe that a gene was missing. Lessons had yet to be learned. I was in dire need of more Biblical passages.

BY THE time 1963 came around, most of us were 16 and driving, giving us the freedom to go places we never before dreamed possible. We went on dates, cruised to combos, and searched for parties where alcohol was involved. Way underage and unable to buy on our own, off we went on Friday and Saturday nights to parts unknown.

BGA boarding student Andy Mitchell was spending a weekend at my house in the fall of 1963 when he mentioned that another boarder, Joe Shapard, and some other upperclassmen, were having a party at the Hotel Savoy on Seventh Avenue North, in downtown Nashville. There was to be lots of beer. This was great—a new adventure in a hotel. Unfortunately, the Savoy had seen its heyday some years earlier. Andy and I entered the lobby and headed to the elevator to go to the fourth floor. We passed a grizzled individual dozing in the corner and another scruffy fellow squirting Cheez Whiz on a saltine cracker. This gave us good vibes—Cheez Whiz was known to be a delicacy in mobile-home parks. Exiting the elevator, we ran into Shapard and his friends coming in and out of a room overlooking an alley. He said, "Grab a beer. They're in the bathtub." Sure enough, there they were—cans and cans of beer floating in ice with a handy church key resting on the sink.

The Hotel Savoy was located on 7th Avenue North. It had seen better days by the time the author visited in the 1960s. (Mike Slate)

This advertisement for the Peppermint Lounge and the Black Poodle appeared in the April 6, 1963, Nashville Banner. (Tennessee State Library and Archives)

We thought it couldn't get any better than this; free beer for us underage kids, a hotel room all our own, and friends to party with.

About that time someone yelled: "Raid!" Guys started running out of the room, leaving Andy and me with a tub full of Pabst. A couple of boys climbed out onto the window ledge while we crouched behind the door by the commode. This was some party. After several minutes of silence, we scurried out to the stairwell and made it to the first floor in about five seconds, blowing past the Cheez Whiz derelict and out the front door, all without being captured. We never learned if there was a raid or not, only that Hotel Savoy was now a place we would never enter again.

Being a long way from age 21, the right to buy alcohol legally caused problems for us teens. Many wanted to go to Printer's Alley to the VooDoo

Room, or The Peppermint Lounge at the Black Poodle, but that was out. A strict policy of 21-and-over-only was observed. So we had to figure a way around it. At BGA, we were required to take Mrs. Reddick's typing class, as part of being well-rounded. If you averaged a B grade in that class (my high-water mark), you were allowed to take your study hall in the typing room and use it during any vacant period. Andy, who was from Georgia, and I devised a way to alleviate all this underage oppression: He would pose as a school official and write to the Georgia Department of Transportation requesting hundreds of blank driver licenses to be used as instructional tools for young students to learn how to properly fill out the cards. We could then make up birth dates and sell them. Now we would get our own fake I.D.s and make some money to boot. It was a shot in the dark, for sure. The state employee to whom the letter found its way must have been one of their top minds, because several weeks later, a package arrived addressed to Andrew Mitchell at Battle Ground Academy from the GDOT, with hundreds of blank licenses. They even thanked us for the request. We were in business, completely unaware

Village Market, which was located on 21st Avenue South between Peabody and Blakemore, is pictured here in 1957. (Metro Archives)

of the felonious nature of what we were about to do. Study halls and after-school hours became a typing frenzy. Mrs. Reddick thought we were quite conscientious.

We spread the word, and most every high-schooler got wind of it. Kids who were underage were now 21 or 22. Height, weight, color of eyes and hair were related to us for transference to their new Georgia driver's license. After several weeks of this, and at $20 a license, we even had plans of a franchise. It was related to me that one Overton student flashed his I.D. at the Village Market in Hillsboro Village and got this response from the manager: "Son, you sure don't look 21. You know I have seen an awful lot of kids from Georgia in here lately."

The pick-up spot was my parents' mailbox, not a smart move because our neighbor, Mrs. Slabosky, noticed a regular flow of cars opening our mailbox and decided to question my mother. Uh-oh. Ugly details aside, this ended the I.D. caper. A good thing we were caught by parents rather than authorities, because I heard that Jordonia School for Boys was not a church camp. I received the wrath of my mother, but Andy, being from out of state, got off without his folks ever knowing. I need to locate his next of kin.

My grandparents lived just a mile or so from campus, so I would occasionally walk over to their place after school to visit. My granddaddy kept cold bottles of Falstaff and Pabst Blue Ribbon in the refrigerator for refreshment after long days at his law office. One afternoon no one was home except Inky, their dog, and all that cold beer. I figured with 12 bottles, taking three was no big deal, and for sure Inky wouldn't tell. Enjoying those forbidden beverages on this hot afternoon, prior to an unofficial basketball scrimmage back at school, was just the thing. I slugged three down, stumbled across the L&N railroad at the end of their lot, and made it back to Briggs Gymnasium just in time to join in the game. It only took a couple of minutes before I started sweating Falstaff. Comments such as "Someone smells like a horse in here" raised eyebrows, and nostrils. Let us say my court awareness became compromised. Dizzy Dean would have been proud.

My granddaddy also raised eyebrows, back in 1937, when John Sharp Williams, a distinguished senator from Mississippi, came to Franklin to visit his old roommate at the University of Virginia, lawyer John H. Henderson,

Melfi's drive-in restaurant, located on 20th Avenue South, in 1959. One could drive up in the back of the building, flash an I.D. and get served alcohol while in your car. (Frank Melfi)

my great grandfather. An account was published in The Nashville Tennessean in 1937 by T. H. Alexander. The story goes that Williams had gone back to their old dorm room at UVA, and a young student named Henderson lived there and entertained him for a few days.

He said to my granddad's father, "Do you know that scamp drank me under the table every night? I never did see a boy drink so much liquor. Do you know Henderson, from somewhere in Tennessee?"

"Yes, I know him", said the elder Mr. Henderson, grimly, "He's my son."

I took after my granddaddy.

Visiting my grandparents in Franklin every Sunday was a family ritual. One particular Sunday, back in 1963, I decided to stay home with some pals, shoot some ball on our backyard court, and watch a favorite show of mine, "Fractured Flickers" with host Hans Conried and his cast of characters: Rocky J. Squirrel, Bullwinkle J. Moose, Mr. Peabody and his WABAC ("way back") Machine, Hoppity Hooper, Snidley Whiplash and others. Shortly after my folks left, here comes Ed, Billy and the guys with a bottle of Gordon's Gin that Billy said he got from his yardman. Gordon's slogan was "Four Ways the English Keep Cool." Hey, we were English. After passing the bottle around, out we went for a little friendly game of hoops. Truth be told, I was the only one who could really play; the others, after several slugs of firewater, thought they could. An hour of imbalance on the concrete and it was time to call in Dr. Kildare. I cleaned out all the Band-Aids, mercurochrome and iodine in the house. As my pals left limping and scraped up, taking the half-full gin bottle with them, I yelled the line Conried used to describe the show: "This is what we will be doing for the next several weeks—or until someone finds out!" Someone found out…about the gin. The show continued, the "fractured" basketball did not.

Just the title "Vacation Bible School" set off red flags to me. How could kids have a vacation when you had to go to school and study Bible verses? Besides, we could watch Ira North and "Know Your Bible" on WSIX television and learn all about those verses. The answer is you really couldn't, except at certain church retreats. Most every church had these overnight stays for teens, so they could enjoy the surroundings and practice Christian fellowship.

United Church of Christ had one of these retreats, back in 1964 at Montgomery Bell State Park, in the Dickson community. Howard (fictitious name to protect the guilty) had affection for a pretty Overton High co-ed who had drawn his attention in Sunday school class. It just so happened that both sets of parents signed the kids up for the retreat. Howard suddenly became a fan of the Gospel. A shy lad, he had never expressed his feelings toward the lass and never would have if somebody hadn't introduced Southern Comfort to the mix. My guess is that it was purchased with one of those fake Georgia driver's licenses, or stolen out of the pastor's suitcase. Mind you, no date, no prior phone calls, nor much of any conversation had ever taken place between the two, but with this intoxicating spirit involved, true feelings came out.

"Southern Comfort should have been called Southern Courage," Howard said, "because after a few slugs of that elixir, I thought I was Cary Grant, and began professing my love for the girl. Love becomes an easy word to say when you are plotzed."

After rattling off sonnets that would make Lolita blush, he was walked back to his cabin by a mortified adult and experienced an epic hangover the next day. I'm sure rumors of underage drinking and love-making on the retreat increased applications for the next summer. As for that gal? She became a

THE ELLIS SPECIAL

A LIGHT BLEND OF SEVEN INGREDIENTS FOR THE PIZZA GOURMET'S PALATE!

GROUND BEEF — BACON — MUSHROOMS — ONIONS
SPANISH OLIVES — HOT GREEN PEPPERS — PEPPERONI
(No substitutions will be made)

Small	Medium	Large
$2.85	$4.15	$5.15

This detail of a House of Pizza menu shows The Ellis Special pizza. The author and other underage friends would add extra garlic and onions in hopes of disguising the alcohol on their breaths.

Mouseketeer on our local Mickey Mouse Club. Howard? That was his last church retreat...hallelujah.

After some beer, it was almost routine for several of us boys and girls to go to the House of Pizza on White Bridge Road. Running mate Dave and I usually ordered the Ellis Supreme, with extra onion and garlic, to disguise the alcohol on our breath. Marge, Dave's mom, said to him one morning, when she opened the door to his room, "I know you kids have been drinking, but for Christ's sake, quit eating the onion and garlic pizza."

We cut back out of respect.

Many restaurants unknowingly catered to underage kids. Ireland's, across from Vandy, was notorious. My pal Goldie put it this way: " It was very dark in there and hard to see young underage guys like me sitting in those cushy booths. Nothing was better than sipping an ice cold Budweiser, eating a Roastburger served on a French roll, with an order of fries on the side, while listening to The Impressions sing 'Keep on Pushing' from the Seeburg jukebox. Our regular waiter was named Mayfield, no relation to Curtis. After feeling the zest of the libations and soulful sounds, it was over to the pinball machine, a beautiful 1962 Bally Miss America. Margaret, the grumpy old cashier, would pay you cash if you racked up enough games. What more could a 16-year-old ask for? Great beer, great music, great food, and illegal gambling and drinking, all under one roof."

Melfi's, the first to offer pizza in Nashville and where the waiters would serve you curbside around back, was just down the road off 21st Avenue. This was very cool when you were in your mom's car with your underage date by your side. Goldie recalls: "I would show my fake Virginia I.D. [I guess some other kids were in the business], order one of the best pizzas in town with a six-pack of Miller High Life, turn on WLAC radio, sit back and listen to the Hossman play Garnett Mimms, and just see what happens."

It was more fun than a church retreat.

Those "duck-and-cover" drills in the 1950s and '60s in schools, to practice shielding ourselves from a nuclear attack, initiated a construction boom in home bomb shelters. My BGA classmate Calvin Hougland had one in a field in front of his family home on Old Hickory Boulevard. After the crisis died down somewhat, the shelter became a party spot one weekend back in 1964. Some Franklin high co-eds, my pal Bert and I and others devised a way to stay out all night with PGA as the catalyst. PGA was the abbreviation for 190 proof "pure grain alcohol," a high-end bay rum without the fragrance of your local barber shop. It was a great mixer, and could be bought at a liquor store with a fake I.D. Enough of that flammable liquid and you barked at the moon, on all fours. Calvin mixed his own using "a few drops out of every bottle in my parent's bar." This night, Bert was to sleep at my house, and I was to stay at his. Fool-proof we thought. Well, sir, that PGA and juice was spread

Pictured as it looks today, this bomb shelter was the scene of some teenage shenanigans in the '60s. *(Calvin Hougland)*

around underground for most of the evening, and who did what with whom or where we all ended up is a blurred memory. However, I can say "duck and cover" took on a whole new meaning. No bomb hit until the next day when we arrived back at our homes. Unbeknownst to us, my mom had called Bert's mom and said I had forgotten an essential item, probably a toothbrush or a clean pair of Fruit-of-the-Looms, to which Bert's mom said she thought we were at my house. Yikes. In addition to suffering from a severe case of the PGA flu, we both were punished with lengthy incarcerations. Later, I was told, there was some barking at the moon, but, thank the Holy spirits, it wasn't me.

Stories, such as girls running half naked across the new Harpeth Hills golf course in 1965, with cherry vodka in their veins, are a lot of fun to remember, but there are too many to tell. Underage drinking was a new adventure for us Boomers and caused uninhibited behavior. One kid who practiced both stated: "Getting liquor was never a problem; getting caught was the problem."

I think it might be fun to go back to one of those weekends when we were teens in the 1960s, if there was only a way to do it. Hey, Mr. Peabody, do you still have your "WABAC Machine"?

CHAPTER 18

Hideouts

I AM NOT sure what motivates youngsters to find places to hide, but I suspect that during my time and before it had something to do with nursery rhymes, stories of Injun Joe's hideout, and Tom Sawyer and Becky Thatcher's cave. For sure, Tarzan's tree house, the Little Rascal kid's club houses and early radio and television shows had an influence. Maybe it was just something that was part of a Southern kid's life, but whatever precipitated it, fun times ensued.

Having two older sisters had its benefits. One was no hand-me-downs. I had no interest in riding girl bikes, playing with girlie toys, such as dolls and play kitchens, and, for gosh sakes, I had no desire to wear feminine clothes—much to the relief of my dad. But there was one thing that my sisters had that I did have some fun with, and that was a large, brown-and-white log playhouse. They used this outdoor "doll house" (as my dad called) for 10 years before I came on the scene. The one-room

The author sits on the porch of his sisters' log playhouse in 1948.

The author (right) and other kids dig in dirt mound in alley way in 1954. The scrapbook caption for the photo: "We'll have it fixed today!" "What is it? A series of holes that lead to nowhere."

structure came complete with a porch and small chairs. It was even big enough for an adult to walk into, provided he did an exaggerated hunch.

How it physically got into our back yard was not clear to me, but it was probably by way of an alley that ran the entire block, behind houses on Westmont and Lynnbrook Roads. These paths were used for garbage and brush pick up. We believe it was off-loaded from the alley directly to the farthest spot in the corner of our property. From about 1943 until sometime around 1950, both my sisters entertained kids from all over the neighborhood in that little hideaway. Tea parties, hide-and-seek headquarters, and just playing house was the thing. Avoiding wasps was all part of the experience. Oldest sis had the misfortune of getting stung by some one day, only because, she said, "I provoked them."

By the time the '50s came along, my siblings were beyond playing house. I used it from age 4 until age 7. I also provoked insects in 1953; however, the ones I irritated were bumble bees, who let me have it five times before I could scurry away. My friends and I would use that miniature log home for a hideout, similar to what we saw on those old TV westerns on Saturdays.

According to my oldest sister, she believed the demise of the playhouse was because my dad wanted to build a barbecue pit where it sat. I was 6 years old in January 1953 when it disappeared. Its end was recorded in the caption of a photo in a family scrapbook: "The last days of the doll house."

I hate to admit it, but some unsupervised "playing doctor" caused the local authorities (my parents) to close it down. All of us unlicensed practitioners were brought up before the ethics committee and reprimanded. So went the doll house.

The next year, in the Haurys' lot behind our back yard, appeared an area of mystery. It was a large pile of dirt containing some openings that had been unloaded for some project we knew nothing about. Inspired by Tom Sawyer, Becky Thatcher, and their cave exploits, it gave us youngsters hope that there was such a cavern within that mountain. We dug and dug until we couldn't dig anymore. We finally figured out we were not going to find an underground hideout. What were we thinking?

There were big closets upstairs in my home, where one of my sister's bedrooms was located, and where I would eventually take up residence. One closet in particular was in an alcove. Opening up the small door, you were faced with a long rack of clothes, all hanging in front of you. But there was a neat feature: if you pushed aside the garments, a little room with benches on each side would be revealed. It was cool and a perfect hideout. A single light was located in the center of this space with a plug for my radio as well. I could go in there, push the clothes back, and be completely hidden in my own little area. That is until my mother would holler up the stairs for me to come to supper. She knew where I was.

Just trying to be hidden and to have my own little spot became an obsession. All kids seemed to mirror my feelings back then. TV was in its infancy, so kids had to be ingenious and inventive. Everyone made tent hideouts using sheets and our parents' furniture, particularly on rainy days. I remember one in our den that was so expansive folks had to go around to the front door to enter our house. I think we used five sheets, several quilts and numerous bedspreads. Underneath were several foot stools, sofa pillows , and a tall hat rack in the middle, just to give it that professional look. We kidnapped my dog Red and used him as a lookout. He left quickly, collapsing several rooms as he scampered out of the enclosure.

Our basement provided a clubhouse for several of us boys. Kids needed a clubhouse to set up rules, strategize, and to plot neighborhood adventures, just like the Little Rascals used to do in their clubhouse. They had a "gang" called the He-Man Woman Haters Club, no girls allowed. I wasn't that stringent. Ours was set up on the back side of the steps. It was barricaded by the underpinnings of the house, a ground level window, a shelf containing paint, tools and laundry detergent, and a long table used for sorting clothes. There was one chair, where the yardman sat and changed into his work gear, that we used as well.

My recollection is that just when we were in a secretive planning mode, down the steps would come mother with a load of laundry. It sort of ruined the atmosphere. Besides that, the mustiness and dust from the coal bin and furnace irritated the sinuses. So much for the underground hideout.

Back outside, tree houses provided probably the best hideout ever devised. They dotted my neighborhood back in the 1950s. As far back as the first century, during the Roman era, Pliny the Elder described such a recreational house for Caligula, as being of the "platform kind." These structures provided protection from the heat, predators, floods, and enabled the inhabitants to see for long distances. They were watchtowers. In more modern times, Winston Churchill built one 20 feet up in a lime tree. I really can't see ole Winston scaling the trunk.

Four blocks away from my home on Cantrell Avenue, at 701 Clearview Drive, grade-school classmate Paul Clements got into the act. With no construction skills, his tree house idea fell to their yardman, Felix King, in 1953. Felix put up a permanent ladder for easy climbing, fashioned a rail around the eight-foot high structure, made sure it was properly supported by four-by-four corner posts, and nailed it to a couple of nearby trees.

But, according to Clements, the real gem was constructed solely by his adopted cousin, Livingston Kelly, in 1961. It was perched 20 feet up in a big hackberry tree, had plywood sides, two separate rooms and a roof.

"Livingston painted the whole thing green," Clements said.

It was a camouflaged hideout. On top of that, there was no ladder, making

Sam Herbert's tree house, built by him when he was only 7, was located behind his house and not far from his brother's tree house. Pictured is his brother Charlie in 1954. (Sam Herbert)

it a real chore for grown-ups to check on the kids.

"Getting up there required jumping up, grabbing a lone horizontal limb that was about eight feet off the ground, and pulling yourself up into a sitting position," Clements said. "Then it was a matter of climbing up wherever convenient branches grew out from the tree, until you got up to the tree house."

That house made it into the 1970s, and parts were still visible into the 1980s. Clements states that the tree came down around 2010. I hope there was a ceremony.

On my street was built a tree house in an old willow, next to a creek, in the back of a lot, at the home of the Elder family at 919 Cantrell Ave. Its childhood occupants included Randy, his sister, and his older brother, Robin. It was built, not by "Pliney the Elder," but by Randy's father, Charles the Elder, around 1948. It was 12 to 15 feet off the ground and included two windows. It was located next to a vacant piece of land where Woodmont school kids came for carnivals, haunted houses and other events put on there by the

Elder clan. There was a chicken coop, complete with fryers just waiting for Mrs. Elder to wring their necks and serve up a tasty weekday supper. What a setting. The tree house had no proper entrance, only some tree knots for grabbing. Once you were up there and wanted to get down, Randy would often hear someone say, "I dare you to jump" or "I double-dog dare you to jump." No word how many ambulance calls were made.

It is said Robin had a cape and often frightened the little kids by riding on top of a garbage truck as it motored down the hill. With the cape fluttering in the wind, the spectacle must have resembled Count Dracula on the loose. I can only imagine what it looked like to a 4 or 5 year old when he leaped from the tree house. When Robin outgrew the lofty hideout, young Randy and his pals took over until approximately 1958, when all the double-dog daring ended and the kids moved on to bigger and better things.

During this time, and across the side street from our home, was Herbert's Field, whose eastern boundaries meshed into four backyards of what we all called "Herbert's Row." In the backyard of the Johnny Herbert home, at the boundary to the field, oldest son Charlie built a large tree house with the help of his dad, in 1948. Constructed based on plans Charlie had drawn up on the back of a brown paper sack, it was hammered together in the clutches of a

Charlie Herbert's tree house, built with the help of his father, is shown at left under construction in 1949 and at right after completion. The strong construction helped fortify it during neighborhood mud ball wars. (Sam Herbert)

cherry tree near third base of Herbert's Field. It had burlap window shades, was symmetrical in appearance and well fortified. Good thing it was, because it took regular poundings from mud ball wars during neighborhood skirmishes.

When younger brother Sam turned 7 in 1954, he, too, wanted a tree house like his brother's. He started to build one in a huge hackberry "north of Charlie's." Judging from its curb appeal, Alfalfa, Porky, Buckwheat and the gang could have put it together.

"Charlie was 7 years older and therefore better schooled than me in construction, plus I was a little kid," Sam said. "And he also had help. I was 7. Maybe that accounts for my poor workmanship. I guess you would call it function over form."

The two tree houses of both brothers were up at the same time. Sam's "eyesore" probably came down prior to 1957, because of what he said were "too many branches coming through the roof." That same year, Sam moved into his brother's room while Charlie went off to college at Georgia Tech.

Tree houses, while providing a great private place for kids, can be places of peril if not respected. Sam relates this near-tragic catastrophe in the fall of his sixth grade with friend Frederic Billings.

"Frederic and I were working on a mad scientist experiment after school in Charlie's old tree house. I was sick one day and begged off to my mother, who let me stay home from school," Sam said. "By afternoon, I was feeling better, probably because the sun was shining, and I told mother I needed to go help Frederick, who was in the tree house. That didn't work, so I had to resume my convalescence. Later, I happened to look out my bedroom window just as a ball of fire fell out of the trap door, with Frederick not far behind. He stomped out the flames but only singed his PF Flyers [tennis shoes]."

Thank goodness for that. I always suspected those chemical sets of Mr. Wizard (a TV show starring, coincidentally, Don Herbert) were not all they were cracked up to be.

By the late 1950s and into the 1960s, most of us kids had moved on to more "mature" adventures. Unfortunately, Charlie was killed at Harding Road and Belle Meade Boulevard in a single car accident while home from college in 1959.

Most of us never saw those tree houses come down. Just as well, I suppose.

No more skinned knees and scraped elbows from the rough bark, or twisted ankles from ill-advised aerial departures from 20 feet. And those clubhouses and hideouts in our parents' living rooms, dens, basements and closets returned to being just that—dens, closets, basements and living rooms.

As for the trees we played in, most have been cut down for the sake of progress. It's possible you might find an old hackberry, willow or maple tree twisting in the breeze somewhere with the remnants of a board or two rotting away, but they are few and far between. Should you happen to find one, how about reflecting back to the good time kids had in those trees. I double-dog dare you.

CHAPTER 19

Old-Time Religion

COMING FROM a devoutly Christian family, I was destined for a proper upbringing. All the ingredients were there, because my early descendents were committed, God-fearing church-goers who passed on that old-time religion to both sets of grandparents and, ultimately, to my parents. My sisters and I were raised as Methodists and assimilated into West End Methodist Church, where my folks influenced countless souls with their unyielding faith.

Let it be known that there is no questioning their commitment, for I was a faith-testing youngster.

West End, as I knew it, was built in 1940, directly across from Vanderbilt University. From 1946, and every Sunday morning from the early 1950s until the mid-1960s, I was required by my mother to attend Sunday school at 8:30 a.m., followed by what I called "Big Church" at 11 a.m. After four hours of repentance, my siblings and I (with my neatly combed hair,

The author, surrounded by his sister Lynn, his mother and his sister Beth, are pictured in 1953. He has been "shined up" for church. The caption on the original photo, written by his father, says, "Look at Tom's hair!"

The West End Methodist Church is pictured circa 1959, when the author was in attendance. See our March 2012 issue for the original 1940 Nashville Banner article about its completion. (West End Methodist Church Archives)

a tie that was always too tight, and freshly-polished shoes) were frequently rewarded with a trip to the local Centennial Park or treated to a Sunday lunch at a nice restaurant, such as the Surf, Bozeman's or sometimes down at the Hermitage hotel for their buffet. In later years, my dad got out of going to Sunday school. How that happened I'll never know. I give him a great deal of credit for accomplishing that feat. I was not as fortunate.

Not only were Sunday school and Big Church a part of the regimen, but in my early teen years it was also mandatory that I attend the Sunday evening MYF (Methodist Youth Fellowship) program. As far as I was concerned, this was a program for teenagers to gather with kids they rarely saw during the week (at least in my case, for I went to an out-of-town school), sit in hard-back wooden chairs in a church classroom, analyze biblical passages and then trudge down to McWhirter Hall (the lunchroom and meeting area of the church) for additional socializing and nibbling on finger sandwiches and sipping non-alcoholic refreshments. At age 16, I thought slugging down a Colt 45 Malt or downing a tea glass full of communion wine would have livened-up the night; however, that wasn't to be. I would rather have been in a dance class figuring out how to do the bossa nova or the polka.

I should note that a lot of girls liked the teenage program, because they could meet new guys, and at some churches, such as Belmont Methodist and Calvary, they could even attend dances. As for me, I think I griped enough to finally have this requirement lifted, probably because a thorough questioning of the evening events when I got home received no specific answers, continually raising suspicion that I had slipped out of the meetings. God had mercy on me.

The practice of attending Sunday services was not waived while on vacation, unfortunately. My mother, who must have invented the GPS system, could always come up with a nearby Methodist church for us to attend. It was mind-boggling how she could locate them. We filled out many guest registration forms for coastal houses of worship. Fortunately, Sunday school and MYF attendance were not enforced while we were out of town, or I would have been pictured nationwide on various milk cartons.

When kids are disinterested, or are required to participate in things they are not fond of, all sorts of abnormal conduct can result. Cases in point:

In a West End Methodist Sunday school class students work on craft projects, circa 1955. (West End Methodist Church Archives)

the song by Ray Stevens, "The Mississippi Squirrel Revival," relates the story of a child who releases a wild squirrel inside his grandparent's church in Pascagoula, Miss.; and similarly there's the tale of kids unleashing angry yellow jackets in a rural sanctuary, forcing worshipers to flee their Sunday services.

Good friend and neighbor Bill Baker told me of the time his actions closely resembled the bedlam of the yellow-jacket fiasco when, as a young lad, he was "removed" from the Sunday school class that his mother required him to attend. One Sunday morning, after repeated corrections by the teacher, Bill was told to leave the room, which he did, but not by conventional means. He squeezed out a side window, much to the disgruntlement of his instructor, but to the laughter of all the kids. Now walking outside the church facility, killing time before Big Church began at 11 a.m., he noticed that a long, street-level window leading to the basement of the building was opened just wide enough for a kid to crawl through. An adventurous boy, he did just that. Once inside, he quickly figured out it was the storage area for the kitchen, complete with an enormous fan attached to several tentacles of duct work leading upwards to the main facility. Rummaging around amongst all the condiment and cooking supplies, he came across an industrial-size vat of ground pepper that a worker had mistakenly left uncapped. Surmising that the fan circulated air throughout the entire building, including the sanctuary, he came up with a plan to get even with the crotchety teacher and the church for

The author and his sisters are pictured outside a Galveston, Texas, hotel in 1953. The author was not happy that his mother had found a church for them to attend while on vacation.

A West End Methodist candle-light service pictured circa 1963, as viewed from the balcony. (West End Methodist Church Archives)

kicking him out of class. Using a large dipping ladle, he plugged in the fan and proceeded to sling large quantities of black pepper into the whirring blades. After emptying half the container, he immediately scampered back out of the window and eventually met his folks upstairs for the 11 a.m. service.

Not long after "How Great Thou Art" or one of the other opening hymns had been sung, the minister and several communicants in the front row began to sneeze and cough, followed by more in the adjoining pews. Eventually most of the congregation began a panicked, sneezing, eye-watering exodus out into the street. Police and firemen were alerted and dispatched to the scene. Fearing a mass chemical exposure was in progress, they arrived with wet towels and wearing gas masks. Bill, now out on the sidewalk with his folks and hacking worshipers, cracked a sly smile but never told anyone. Services were cancelled for the rest of the day and the church was fumigated and thoroughly cleaned. Newspaper accounts speculated for weeks as to the cause, but nothing was ever

The Elliston Place Soda Shop is shown in 1955. Being located near West End Methodist Church made it a good hideout for the author during Sunday school.

directly attributed to the caustic irritation and mass evacuation. Decades later, the church secretary was asked by my straight-faced friend if they ever figured out what happened that day when everyone about choked to death during church service. Her answer was: "No, son, we never knew what happened." The Great Sneeze-Out Caper remains in that church's lore to this day.

Between the ages of 12 and 16, I was never kicked out of Sunday school class, primarily because a couple of us would rarely make an appearance. Elliston Place Soda Shop was just a block or so down the street, making for a perfect spot to hide and slurp down a shake and kill 45 minutes. Some of the hung-over folks we saw in there on Sunday mornings gave us a lesson in vocabulary we would have never received in Sunday school. Most Sundays, I was queried by my mother as to what I had learned in class. I for sure couldn't tell her that I picked up another curse word at the soda shop. I usually replied with something like: "Jesus told Zacchaeus to get down out of the Sycamore tree," or cited any biblical reference that might indicate I had broadened my religious knowledge. I could relate to Zacchaeus, because I was often told to get down out of our tulip poplar and come to supper.

Other times, a friend and I would roam concealed passageways and basement level tunnels that were part of West End's expansive structure. One door led down an unlit staircase to McWhirter Hall and a backstage, and another led to the rear entrance of the choir loft. Hiding behind a tall curtain, we made soft, squeaky noises, often distracting some vocalists in the back row, which frequently caused a scowling head turn. That was a great reward to a couple of mischievous kids. This was a quiet time throughout the church, with no one stirring much except kids evading Sunday school—no one, that is, except Mrs. Perry. She was a sweet, but stern, short, dumpy lady who must have been hired by "Dragnet's" Joe Friday, or the church hierarchy, to tail me every week. Coming around a darkened stairwell and bouncing into her put the fear of God into us kids.

"Tommy, I am going to have to tell your mother," she would say. The Lord had a way, I guess.

Once the main church service began, and during the time I was a young teen, my parents and I sat in the balcony overlooking the sanctuary. It was an impressive sight, peering over the rail and seeing all the worshipers filling up each and every pew. Eventually, I moved a spot higher up and off to the side of my folks with a friend or two whose family also sat in the balcony. Not paying much attention to the sermons by Bishops Henley, Short, St. Clair, Clark, and the rest who graced that holy pulpit way down below, I would often grab the short pencil from the slot on the rear of the pew in front of me and make lists on the backs of pledge envelopes of neighborhood kids to call when I got home. I would divide them into equal teams for a Sunday afternoon ball game and make either positive or derogatory remarks as to their talent level beside their name. Who knows what the ushers thought when they replaced those cards after every service. Having to sit for an hour, this activity did not consume enough time, and Bobby, Burton, Jimmy and I became bored. I was good at improvising and noticed that my clip-on, Rayon tie had feather-like pieces of wispy, silky threads that were concealed between the overlapping fabric on the underside (talk about being bored). I determined that you could slowly pull each thread out one at a time, place it on your finger, and blow it up into the air. These threads were so light that the circulating current would catch them and float them upwards, until they eventually drifted slowly down, either on or in front of folks in the pews below us. At one point, with several of us in the act, it looked as if a brief snowfall was taking place. We watched as an elderly couple, in the pew in front of us, glanced upward and then proceeded to brush off the clinging strands from their clothes. The husband leaned over to his wife and what we heard was something to the effect of, "Where in the Hell is all this crap coming from?" right after this stanza of "Amazing Grace":

> *Amazing Grace, how sweet the sound,*
> *That saved a wretch like me*
> *I once was lost, but now am found,*
> *Was blind, but now, I see.*

Evidently what he saw was not to his liking. It was all we could do to hold the giggling down. The sad thing is we were never caught. Only God knew. I guess that is all that matters. I should have said a prayer for that poor wretch.

I must say thanks to my mother, because the days I spent in Big Church, and the times I did show up in Sunday school, I managed to become instilled with a Godly spirit that is with me to this day. Had I not been dragged there, I would never have seen the glorious Christmas Eve candlelight service, been able to recite the 23rd Psalm or sing at a glass-breaking pitch the hymn "Holy Holy Holy." Nor would I have learned "The Lord's Prayer" without a hymnal in front of me or been able to repeat this Benediction without skipping a beat:

> *The LORD bless you and keep you;*
> *The LORD make His face shine upon you, And be gracious to you;*
> *The LORD lift up His countenance upon you, And give you peace.*

For sure, I would have never known that someone by the name of Zacchaeus climbed trees like me. To all of that, I say a big "Amen!"

ABOUT THE AUTHOR

Tom Henderson III is a native Nashvillian, born at the old St. Thomas Hospital and raised in the Woodmont Hills section of town. He attended his neighborhood elementary school, Woodmont, went to high school at Battle Ground Academy in Franklin, Tenn., and is a graduate of Memphis State University.

He is a U.S. Army Medical Corps veteran, serving our country from 1966–1969, including one year in Vietnam.

He has been writing a monthly nostalgia column for "The Nashville Retrospect" since the publication's inception in 2009. He has also written for the "Williamson County Historical Society Journal" and is a frequent moderator, panelist, and presenter at the Green Hills Historic Homecoming events.

Tom was featured in the highly-acclaimed Nashville Public Television production "Nashville: The 20th Century in Photographs," volumes one and two.

In 2016 he spoke at the annual Southern Festival of Books.

Tom is the author of the locally best-selling books "When I Was a Kid: Growing up in Nashville from the '40s to the '70s" and "Yesterdays: A Nashville Kid Recalls the Best of Times." Both are popular Baby Boomer flashback books that relive everything from going to drive-in movies, cruising, dancing to combos in driveways, walking to the local drug store, shopping downtown, and skating at the roller rink, to doing the laundry, riding around with the milk man, stoking the coal furnace, going to those make-out parties, and being mischievous…plus most everything in between.

His speaking and slide-show presentations continue to be popular attractions with civic organizations, alumni groups and historical institutions across the city.

He has two older sisters, has been married since 1967, and still lives in Nashville. He has three sons and a bunch of grandkids.

Tom Henderson III

Made in the USA
Columbia, SC
19 October 2017